PORTFOLIO
PAY IT DOWN!

Jean Chatzky is the financial editor for NBC's *Today*, a contributing editor for *More* magazine, a columnist for *New York Daily News*, and a contributor to *The Oprah Winfrey Show*.

She is the author of six books, including *The Difference: How Anyone Can Prosper in Even the Toughest Times* (Crown Business) and the *Wall Street Journal* and *New York Times* best seller *Make Money, Not*

PORTFOLIO

Published by the Penguin Group

Penguin Group (USA) Inc., 375 Hudson Street, New York, New York 10014, U.S.A.
Penguin Group (Canada), 90 Eglinton Avenue East, Suite 700, Toronto, Ontario, Canada
M4P 2Y3 (a division of Pearson Penguin Canada Inc.)
Penguin Books Ltd, 80 Strand, London WC2R oRL, England
Penguin Ireland, 25 St Stephen's Green, Dublin 2, Ireland (a division of Penguin Books Ltd)
Penguin Group (Australia), 250 Camberwell Road, Camberwell, Victoria 3124, Australia (a
division of Pearson Australia Group Pty Ltd)
Penguin Books India Pvt Ltd, 11 Community Centre, Panchsheel Park, New Delhi – 110 017,
India
Penguin Group (NZ), cnr Airborne and Rosedale Roads, Albany, Auckland, New Zealand
(a division of Pearson New Zealand Ltd)
Penguin Books (South Africa) (Pty) Ltd, 24 Sturdee Avenue, Rosebank, Johannesburg 2196,
South Africa

Penguin Books Ltd, Registered Offices: 80 Strand, London WC2R oRL, England

First published in the United States of America by Portfolio, a member of Penguin Group
(USA) Inc. 2004
This edition published in 2009

10 9 8 7 6 5 4 3 2 1

PUBLISHER'S NOTE
This publication is designed to provide accurate and authoritative information in regard
to the subject matter covered. It is sold with the understanding that the publisher is not
engaged in rendering legal, accounting, or other professional services. If you require legal
advice or other expert assistance, you should seek the services of a competent
professional.

LIBRARY OF CONGRESS CATALOGING-IN-PUBLICATION DATA

Chatzky, Jean Sherman, 1964–
    Pay it down! : debt-free on $10 a day / Jean Chatzky. — Rev. ed.
        p. cm.
    Includes index.
    ISBN 978-1-59184-254-5
    1. Consumer credit. 2. Finance, Personal. 3. Debt. I. Title.
    HG3755.C484 2009
    332.024'02—dc22

                            2009031329

Printed in the United States of America

PAY IT DOWN!

Debt-Free
on $10 a Day

Jean Chatzky

PORTFOLIO

*For anyone who
deserves a new beginning*

THE PROMISE: RENEWED

How would you like to be free of overwhelming credit card debt? To have a financial cushion to fall back on? To know you have the skills to save and invest for any goal—and to guarantee your financial future?

I wrote those sentences for the first time six years ago, during more pleasant financial times. The stock market was chugging along nicely. The housing market, doing better than that. Americans were feeling more than flush and as a result many of us were living larger than ever. We outfitted our homes with better appliances, took fancier vacations, added another car to the driveway (or another bay to the garage)—and did it all on borrowed money. Credit cards and home equity lines paved the way. As a country we weren't worried—every time we turned around it seemed that we were wealthier on paper than we had been the day before.

And yet, I had a nagging feeling that this was all a house of cards about to come tumbling down. I felt it for the first time on January 19, 2001. That was the day I opened my *New York Times* to find a story by Louis Uchitelle noting that Americans had less equity in their homes than at any time since the Great Depression. I started digging and found that rising mortgage debt wasn't the only symptom. Fewer of us owned our cars than at any time in the past. Our average household debts on student loans and credit cards were setting new records as well.

And so I dug in to write *Pay It Down!*, a book I was sure Americans were going to need immediately.

I was ahead of my time.

The Rx for getting out of debt laid out in these pages worked then—as it works now. The hundreds of thousands of readers as well as the million people who participated in the Debt Diet on *The Oprah Winfrey Show* (based largely on the information in this book) can attest to that. But too many people weren't ready to listen.

(To show you how ready *you* are to get out of debt, I now have an online program to help you wherever you are at: not ready, getting ready, or ready. This program respects where you are at and works with you to max-imize your success. The program is a result of my col-laboration with James O. Prochaska and Pro-Change and brings the science of behavior change to you. You'll find more information at jeanchatzky.com.)

Then, as the economy twisted and turned, it became clear that only those individuals who minimized their debt and maximized their savings had a shot at a stable financial future. And along the way some of the rules of the road have changed. So I decided to update *Pay It Down!*, because you need different strategies than you needed a mere half decade ago, whether you're trying to:

Negotiate with your creditors

Refinance or modify your mortgage

Increase your credit score

Manage your student loans

Work with a credit counselor

Or simply maintain a decent balance
    between good debt and bad

I give them to you here in the same straightforward, easy-to-stomach way I try to present all of my financial solutions. Life is tough enough without having to wade through pages of unnecessary lingo. And despite the fact that time has passed, the Promise remains the same:

How would you like to be free of overwhelming

credit card debt? To have a financial cushion to fall back on? To know you have the skills to save and invest for any goal—and to guarantee your financial future?

I can give you that. Even in these tough credit markets. Even in this economy. I can give you that for $10 a day. And if that sounds like very little—well, it is.

It's a movie for one, without popcorn.

It's lunch at McDonald's for two children.

It's skipping the car wash and washing the car in your driveway instead.

It's so many of those things that you can do without. But it's also the key to your future. Let's say you're the average American. You have a decent job, but you also have $7,200 in high-rate credit card debt. You have no savings to speak of. You worry about your money on a daily basis (in fact, it keeps you up at night), and you don't believe that $10 a day can dig you out of that hole. But it can, and in less time than you may think. If you get on this plan—and stick with it:

In three years you'll be free of credit cards. By applying that $10 a day against your $7,200 credit card debt (at an interest rate of 16 percent), you'll be debt-free in two years and five months, or twenty-nine months total.

In five years you'll have a financial cushion. Once the debt is gone, you can start saving that $10 a day for your future. You'll put it in a money-market account. It won't earn much in interest while it's sitting there (I used a 2-percent interest rate for this example), but there's no risk you'll lose it either. Five years from the time you started socking away your $10 a day, you'll have a fat emergency cushion—nearly $10,000. That's your insurance against a layoff, an illness, even a leaky roof or other financial mishap that comes your way.

In ten years you'll have a nest egg for retirement. After your emergency cushion is in place, you can start investing your $10 a day so that it can work harder and grow faster for your benefit. If you put it somewhere that it can grow tax-free—such as in a 401(k) account—and you earn, on that money, the 9.44 percent that the S&P 500 has returned between 1926 and today, in ten years (in addition to your emergency cushion), you'll have $23,653; in fifteen years from the day you opened that account, you'll have $61,505; in twenty years, you'll have $122,076; in twenty-five years, you'll have $219,004; in thirty years, you'll have $374,112; in thirty-five years, you'll have $622,323; and in forty years, you'll have $1,019,519.

More than $1 million on $10 a day. Even in these times, these markets, this economy? Yes, even after the last eighteen months, investing for the long term in the

S&P 500 still stands the test of time. The average annual return going all the way back to the Great Depression is 9.44 percent. That's better than bonds, better than cash. That's real money in anybody's book.

It sounds simple, and it is. All that's standing in your way is knowledge. You need to know how to free up that $10 a day. You need to know how to get yourself to do that every day, without fail, for the rest of your life. And you need to know how to guarantee that that money gets to where it's supposed to be so that it can work its magic for you.

The answers are in the next two hundred and fifty pages. Read on.

Contents

Introduction:

Getting Ahead and Staying Ahead

52 million times a day
2.2 million times an hour
36,242 times a minute
604 times a second

That's how often we use our credit cards in this country. That's how often we whip out our slim pieces of plastic and slide them through the little electronic slots or hand them over to the cashier. We type the numbers into our browsers or read them hurriedly to a clerk over the telephone to buy books, groceries, or movie tickets, or even to foot the bill for the copayment at the pediatrician's office. We do it so often, we don't even think about it anymore.

But we should. Because on average, each of those transactions costs us $96. That may not sound like much—dinner for four at the local Italian joint; a sweater and a pair of jeans at the Gap; a rehab for the broken vacuum cleaner—but when we start to add up all of those $96 charges, the number quickly becomes meaningful. And when we lump them with the money we owe on our mortgages, our car loans, our home equity loans, and our student loans, the numbers start to get very large very quickly. In fact, they get downright scary.

The fact is, consumer debt, as measured by the Federal Reserve, reached an all-time high in 2008. Since then, with the economy on the rocks, debt has—thankfully—come down a little bit and simultaneously our country's anemic savings rate has rebounded.

But we are still in an enormous debt hole. The average household in America owes $7,200 on the sixteen—sixteen!—pieces of plastic in our wallets. And credit card debt is just the tip of the iceberg. Over the last decade, loose credit standards enabled us to take out bigger mortgages than we could afford, tap the equity in our homes as if it were a piggy bank, load up on car-loan debt, and saddle ourselves with tens if not hundreds of thousands of dollars in student loans.

And repaying that debt? Well, it became more difficult, thanks to the following one-two punch: Housing values collapsed and the credit spigots dried up.

As a result, not only did we own homes that were worth less than we paid for them—41 percent of mortgages for homes bought in the last five years are now underwater—but we lost our ability to borrow more to keep ourselves afloat.

America's addiction to debt finally caught up with us. And the piper has decided it's time to be paid. That's why some three million Americans have lost their homes to foreclosure as of this writing and another six million are expected to face the process in the next several years. That's why the number of cars repossessed jumped 12 percent in 2008 to 1.7 million and is expected to grow another 5 percent this year. And the number of people filing for bankruptcy—despite the existence of tougher-on-consumer bankruptcy laws since 2005—continues to soar.

Is Debt Getting in the Way of Your Future?

That's the question you have to face down.

If you have too much debt—particularly as compared with your income—I can guarantee that you don't have much of a financial future. Why? Think about what happens when you have bills looming large. Making those payments—the mortgage or rent, the car payment, and, oh, those credit cards (where even the min-imums look maximum)—means there's nothing left over to save or invest. So when an emergency hits, whether it's an unreimbursed medical bill or a new transmission, you pay for it with plastic. Then the min-imums go even higher, and the cycle continues. There are millions and millions of Americans in your shoes.

Are You Ready to Make a Change?

So if you are one of those millions of Americans, I have just one question for you: Are you ready? Are you ready to make a commitment—to get with the program—to right your own financial ship?

Deciding is step zero. It comes before any of the tactical steps that I'll lay out for you in the next two hundred and fifty pages. You have to choose this path. It comes with great rewards: Less worry. Greater com-fort. The knowledge that you are taking better care of yourself as well as the people you love. (If you're not ready, that's okay. As previously mentioned, I now have an online program you can access that respects where you are at and works with that. If you're ready but your partner isn't, the online program could be a good re-source. You can both use it—and the beauty is, you each start where you're at and work at your own pace. You can find more information at jeanchatzky.com.

But you do need to understand that getting on board will require short-term sacrifice. You'll have to give up making purchases unconsciously, buying things you don't need—and often don't even want—just because. Those are, in my opinion and the opinion of so many who have succeeded in Paying It Down, very small prices to pay for lifelong financial independence. But the choice remains yours. And I will tell you this: If you move forward, within a very short while you're not only going to feel optimistic about your financial future; you're going to feel, for the first time in a very long time, as if you really have one.

Pay It Down!

STEP 1

Assess the Problem

How Did You Get into This Mess?

Before you can solve any problem, you need to understand how you got into trouble in the first place. That's the only way you can clear up your mess—in this case, your debt mess—and dramatically reduce your chances of it happening again.

So, I want you to think back. At some point, you had a clean credit record. For some of you, that may have been way back when a solicitor approached you on your college campus and offered you a big bag of M&M's or a T-shirt if you'd apply for a credit card. But for most people, it was sometime after that. Think what was it that sparked the trouble:

Maybe it was when you lost a job. You may be one of the

1

6.7 million (and counting) Americans who've lost a job since the economy turned down in December 2007. Unfortunately, it now takes substantially longer to find a new one than it has in the past. The average person these days is on unemployment for twenty weeks. And even when you do find a new job, it may come at a lower salary, with no health insurance.

Or when you didn't get the raise you were counting on. Perhaps you made a habit of spending ahead of your salary. You figured that although you earned $35,000 this year, you'd earn $40,000 the next year and $45,000 the year after that, so you could afford a more expensive mortgage payment or car payment or wardrobe. But the raises never came—not just for you, but for many people. Since 2000, the average income for a middle-class family hasn't just stagnated—it has actually declined by $2,000. Prices, of course, have continued to rise.

Maybe it was when you bought your house. The house. Of course you always wanted one. And the government wanted you to have one. It's always been the American Dream. But the house as a sure-thing investment has proved to be nothing more than a fallacy: Home prices have fallen 24 percent on average since the market topped out in 2006, and as much as 50 percent in places like Miami, Phoenix, Las Vegas, and parts of California.

Or when you borrowed from said house. Why float the vacation on the credit card when debt in the form of home equity loans and lines of credit was so much cheaper—and tax deductible to boot? That was the prevailing logic for much of the last decade. And while it may have made sense numerically, it allowed too many people to dig themselves into holes that were doubly deep. One third of home equity lines of credit were used to consolidate credit card debts that had become overwhelming. That might have been fine had the borrowers cut up or kept their fingers off the plastic. Instead, 40 percent went out and charged those cards right back up again, which meant that not only did they have big credit card bills; they had put their homes on the line as well.

Or when you rented your apartment. Between 1993 and 2000, rents rose at twice the rate of inflation. They climbed well ahead of the raise you were likely to receive on the job. As your rent ate up a bigger share of your budget each month, maybe you started leaning on your credit cards.

Or when you got divorced. After a divorce, the temptation to try to maintain your standard of living—often by continuing to live in the house you shared with a spouse—is strong. Unfortunately, unless you're independently wealthy, doing so is next to impossible.

Maybe it was when you had a health scare. Forty million Americans have no health insurance. Perhaps you're in that boat, but even if you're not, the rising cost of health care can easily throw you deep into debt. Health-care premiums have skyrocketed in the last decade. Simultaneously, the percentage of people who had employers paying for that health care fell out of the sky.

Maybe you could afford most of these things, but nothing else. Americans have been using their credit cards to fill the gap between how much they earn and how much they need to live. They may be able to pay their rent, their utilities, and their car loans, but groceries, doctors' visits, and other necessities are going on the credit card.

Maybe you had no savings to bail yourself out of a jam. Perhaps the transmission died, or the roof sprung a leak, or you had some other problem that absolutely, positively had to be taken care of, but you had no savings to pay for it. So you had to charge it and figured you'd pay it back later, but the cost of living got in the way.

Maybe you have a spending problem. There are people who are addicted to shopping, and then there are people who just spend more than they make. More and more people every year are falling into the latter category. According to a 2009 Marist poll, 61 percent of families have recently had to cut the family budget dramatically. It's not just luxuries they're doing without. Two thirds are leaving name brands on the shelf to purchase store brands and 64 percent are making their lunch rather than buying it. Unfortunately, if you're spending more than you make, you're digging deeper and deeper into debt.

Maybe It Was a Combination of Things

Now, you may be able to handle one of these problems at a time. But as Murphy's Law would have it, they tend to hit you simultaneously—or sequentially, one right after the other. You could handle the fact that you had a spending problem as long as you had a high-five-figure salary. But then you lost your job. You could handle the fact that you could just barely afford your mortgage payments, until you had a health scare that saddled you with a pile of bills. You thought you could handle the second lease on the second car, until you didn't get that raise you were counting on. I see evidence of that in the e-mails that I receive every single day.

Elizabeth in Washington wrote: "My financial despair

is due in part to a devastating personal loss, which resulted in loss of employment. The loss of my job and the resultant stress of the financial devastation it created further impacted my personal loss. I have been suffering from depression and doing some self-medicating with occasional 'retail therapy.' This behavior worsens my situation and leaves me feeling further overwhelmed by my financial situation. I don't know how to 'get a grip'!"

And from Gloria in Pennsylvania: "Two years ago, my husband was forced to retire after 33 years of employment at a local company. When the 'retirement' occurred, we were in the midst of building an addition [to our home], starting a new business, and paying for my daughter's wedding. We accumulated $17,000 in credit card debt. Our income, since the retirement, is reduced by almost two thirds. Both my husband and I work long hours in a seemingly fruitless attempt to pay down our debt; however, the credit card balances remain almost stationary because of the high interest rates, finance fees, and late fees. We are drowning."

The sort of worry and anxiety that Elizabeth and Gloria express run through just about every one of the e-mails I receive. It also shows up in the results of a 2009 Roper iPoll:

- Some 38 percent of people "worry a lot" about facing major unexpected medical expenses.
- Nearly half "worry a lot" about seeing the value of their stocks and retirement investments drop.
- One third "worry a lot" about being able to keep up with their mortgage and credit card payments.
- More than half are "very worried" about their income not keeping up with rising prices.
- More than one quarter "worry a lot" about losing their job.

Worrying, unfortunately, doesn't do any good; nor does an underlying belief that credit cards are bad or evil. Research by Sue Eccles, a professor at Lancaster University Management School in Great Britain, has shown that most of us believe we use credit too often. Another study by Thomas Durkin, an economist with the Federal Reserve Bank of New York, showed that the more people use their credit cards, the more they feel credit is "bad."

Credit, it turns out, is like a double bacon cheeseburger (with the bun): We know perfectly well that it's bad for us, and yet we eat it anyway.

So, How Bad Is It?

It's time to answer the question, How much debt *do* you have? Many people really don't know, and even if they do, sometimes their spouses don't. (I get e-mails from people who *want* to be "outed" on the radio or on television because they can't tell their spouses that they're hiding a massive credit card bill.)

To get on the road to repayment, you need to know how much debt you're carrying and at what interest rates. And if you're part of a couple, you both need to know.

You can use the worksheet on pages 10 and 11 to get going or you can do the work on a computer or on another piece of paper, but it's time to take stock.

There are two basic types of debts. *Secured debt* is debt that has an asset—also called collateral—backing it up. Your mortgage is a secured debt that uses your house as collateral. If you miss enough mortgage payments, the bank will foreclose and take your house. Your car loan is, similarly, a secured debt. If you stop writing checks to Ford Motor Credit (or whomever), you can count on a visit from the repo man. Likewise, if you've purchased furniture or appliances on a payment plan, you have a secured loan. *Unsecured debt*, on the other hand, is not backed with collateral. Because there are no assets behind unsecured loans, the bank or lender takes a bigger risk in lending you the money. Nothing can be easily taken from you to force you to pay. That's why the interest rates on unsecured loans are higher. Credit card balances are, as you probably figured, unsecured debts.

After you've completed the worksheet your tendency is going to be to worry. Don't. I know your total looks big. I'm going to teach you how to break it down into manageable pieces so that you can tackle it on $10 a day.

Tales of Life and Debt:
"We Didn't Know How Bad It Was"

Until very recently, Tina and Brian, parents of two living in Everett, Washington, could tell you that they were in debt (the bills each month were nonstop and overwhelming), and they could tell you *why* they were in debt (Brian had lost his job as a help-desk analyst nine months earlier, cutting their family income in half). What they couldn't tell you—because they didn't know themselves—was how bad the problem was.

"If I say I didn't want to know, does that make sense?" Tina asked. "I'm kind of scared to figure out where we

SECURED DEBTS

	Lender	Amount Owed	Term	Rate	Fixed or Variable?
Mortgage					
Home equity loan					
Home equity line of credit					
Car loan					
Boat loan					
Furniture/appliance payment					
Time–share					
Other					

Amount Owed Subtotal: $ _____

UNSECURED DEBTS

	Lender	Amount Owed	Term	Rate	Fixed or Variable?
Credit card 1					
Credit card 2					
Credit card 3					
Credit card 4					
Credit card 5					
Credit card 6					
Personal loan					
Other					

Amount Owed Subtotal: $ _____

TOTAL OWED: $ _____

are. Not knowing somehow makes you feel better." Unfortunately, not knowing how much you owe, to whom, and at what interest rate allows you to spend as if the problem doesn't exist, as Tina and Brian had the previous holiday season. It leaves you wondering if you're making the right decisions about whom to pay first. In other words, it gives you room to hang yourself.

There are many, many people in Brian and Tina's situation. According to research conducted for the National Foundation for Credit Counseling in 2008, one third of Americans have absolutely no emergency savings. And of those who do, 57 percent don't have sufficient reserves. That's one big reason that some 34 million Americans told the NFCC they've been late making credit card payments and about 18 million admit they've missed payments entirely. If you're one of the people who are leaning a little too hard on the plastic in their wallets, step one in getting out of debt is understanding why you're in debt and how bad the problem is.

It comes down to basic psychology: If you don't fix the underlying problem, conquering the symptoms will do you no good in the long run. You'll repeat the destructive behavior and end up in the same debt hole all over again. You need to understand why it happened in the first place. The second thing you need to under-stand is how bad the problem is. With my prodding, Tina spent a weekend figuring out how much was com-ing in each month, how much was going out, and where it was going. "It took hours," she said. "I cried."

Tina figured that, with Brian's unemployment checks, they had a net income each month of $4,634. Their aver-age spending for the previous couple of months—which included making the minimum payments on five credit cards, as well as paying the mortgage, a consolidation loan, and home equity line of credit—had been $5,875. "It's even worse than I thought it was," Tina said.

But going through the numbers also showed her the possibilities. Her credit cards were at fairly high interest rates; she vowed to try to reduce those with balance transfers if her existing card companies wouldn't work with her. She also had been spending more than she probably had to for auto and homeowners insurance, as well as for phone service and Internet. She decided she could easily swap from premium cable to cheaper basic, and she'd never thought of contacting the pricey preschool her daughter attended to ask for financial aid.

The family's goal for the next few months was to trim their expenses to the point where they could at least tread water. Brian enrolled in a training program for medical transcriptionists. He'll graduate and, they believe, be back in the workforce within six months. By paring down their spending, they can put themselves in position to make rapid progress on their debt when Brian begins working again. And while daunting, that's a prospect that feels good. "I should have done this years ago," Tina said.

STEP 2

Break Your Challenge into
Manageable Steps

L et's say that instead of trying to get out of debt you were trying to lose a little weight before your high school reunion, two months from now. How would you approach that problem? You'd probably climb on the scale and see that it was teetering around, say, 153. Since all your life you've weighed between 140 and 142, you'd know that you wanted to lose ten pounds. But that's not all you'd know:

- You'd have a goal: to lose weight.
- The goal would be specific: ten pounds.
- You'd have a time frame: before my high school re-union, two months from now.

- You'd have a way to measure how you're doing: the scale.

And because you had that well-defined framework, you'd have a better chance of success—*much better* than if you were simply dieting with no goal and no end in sight.

You need to think of the quest to get out of debt and into wealth in the same way. So we are going to start by focusing on one nagging piece of your debt puzzle: your credit card debt. (You'll find information on reducing your mortgage, student-loan, and car-loan debt loads in Step 5.) Now, I know it's tempting to decide that you're going to get rid of every bit of your credit card debt this year, but you shouldn't aim that high. Why? Because you're not going to be able to do it.

Research from Old Dominion University shows us that when we aim for goals that are beyond our reach, not only do we fail, but we accomplish less than we do when we aim smaller. That's why middle-class people who aim to save smaller amounts actually save more in total dollars than people who set the bar high.

You should know, most people in debt-management programs run by credit-counseling agencies (these are people who are being helped by professionals) take four to five years to emerge debt-free. But I want you to try to do it in three. You'll do this by breaking your big mountain of debt into smaller hills that are actually possible to climb.

In working this way, you do yourself a great service: By giving yourself benchmarks that are actually achievable, you allow yourself to succeed. You'll feel great when you reach each one, and that will make you feel as if you can do even more. If instead you set out to grab the whole enchilada, not only will you feel terrible when you fail (as will likely happen); you won't give yourself the opportunity to do *better* than you anticipate. And that would be a shame.

So here's what your goal looks like broken down:

- You have a goal: to reduce debt.
- It's specific: by $10 a day.
- You have a time frame: debt-free in three years.
- You have ways to measure how you're doing: your balances (and, as we'll see in a little while, your credit score).

Question: What if I have more than the average $7,200 in debt? What if I have $8,000 or more? Answer: To knock off that debt in the same three-year period— which I like because it's neither too short nor too long,

DEBT–FREE IN THREE YEARS

Rate →	12%	16%	18%	20%	24%
Debt					
$8,000	$9/day	$10/day	$10/day	$10/day	$11/day
$10,000	$11/day	$12/day	$12/day	$13/day	$13/day
$12,000	$13/day	$14/day	$15/day	$15/day	$16/day
$14,000	$16/day	$16/day	$17/day	$17/day	$18/day
$16,000	$18/day	$19/day	$19/day	$20/day	$21/day
$20,000	$22/day	$23/day	$24/day	$24/day	$26/day

DEBT–FREE IN FOUR YEARS

Rate →	12%	16%	18%	20%	24%
Debt					
$10,000	$9/day	$10/day	$10/day	$10/day	$11/day
$12,000	$11/day	$12/day	$12/day	$12/day	$13/day
$14,000	$12/day	$13/day	$14/day	$14/day	$15/day
$16,000	$14/day	$15/day	$16/day	$16/day	$17/day
$20,000	$18/day	$19/day	$20/day	$20/day	$22/day
$22,000	$21/dag	$22/day	$22/day	$22/day	$23/day

DEBT–FREE IN FIVE YEARS

Rate →	12%	16%	18%	20%	24%
Debt					
$12,000	$9/day	$10/day	$10/day	$11/day	$12/day
$14,000	$11/day	$12/day	$12/day	$13/day	$14/day
$16,000	$12/day	$13/day	$14/day	$14/day	$16/day
$20,000	$15/day	$16/day	$17/day	$18/day	$19/day
$24,000	$18/day	$19/day	$20/day	$22/day	$23/day
$30,000	$23/day	$25/day	$25/day	$26/day	$29/day

and it gives you plenty of years to build wealth for the future—you have to free up more than $10 a day or decide that four or even five years to financial freedom is okay with you.

I know the numbers in the following Debt–Free charts look discouraging, but I want you to pay very close attention to how much less painful this process is at lower interest rates. The key to being able to grab one of those lower rates is to manage a very important piece of information known as your credit score. We'll talk about that in the next chapter. Then we'll move on to finding the money you need to pay down those bills.

STEP 3

Know and Manage Your Credit Score

If you've ever applied for any sort of credit—a credit card, cellular-phone service, utility service such as gas or electric—then you have:

- A credit history
- A credit report
- A credit score

How did this happen without your knowing about it? Why weren't you consulted?

Sorry, it doesn't work that way. When you went out and applied for your first loan or credit card, you filled out an application. The credit issuer called a credit bureau—probably one of the country's big three, Trans-

Union, Equifax, or Experian—to check up on you, and that bureau, recognizing it didn't have any information on you, started a credit file.

The other bureaus learned about you just a short while later. Let's say the application you filled out was for a credit card. You signed the form, bought a few things, and when the bill came, you paid it. Your credit card company closely monitored how you handled that transaction and sent details on you to all three bureaus, telling them whether you paid on time, what percentage of the outstanding debt you paid, and whether you stayed within your credit limit.

Voilà! You had a credit history. It wasn't very deep or very detailed, but it existed, and each time you paid a bill you padded your file. As you added creditors, the file—and your credit report, which consolidates all the information in your file—grew thicker still. And although some information eventually falls off the report as it ages, much of it follows you around for as long as you have and manage credit—in other words, for the rest of your life.

Six months into your life as a borrower, there was enough information in your file for the credit bureaus to assign you something called a credit score. This is a numerical translation of that credit history that lenders (as well as insurers, employers, landlords, and others) use to make a decision quickly about whether they want to do business with you—and how much to charge if you ever want to do business with them. The score changes all the time as new information about you and your credit behavior is reported to each of the bureaus.

And to say your score is important is an understatement. Although I am a firm believer that we are *not* our credit scores, in recent years they have become a barometer of how responsible a person you are. Each year some 25 billion credit decisions are made based on FICO scores alone. These weren't just decisions about whether applicants would be approved for a new credit card; they also determined:

- How much the applicants could borrow
- What sort of interest rate they would pay
- Whether they qualified for an increase in their credit line
- Whether they qualified to rent an apartment
- Whether they could get a cell phone
- Whether they qualified for a cash advance
- Whether they would actually get the credit card they were "preapproved" for

Your credit history and score also play a role in determining:

- How much you'll have to pay for homeowners and auto insurance. Insurers have discovered that how and whether you pay your bills is more indicative of the number of claims you'll file than your driving record.
- Whether or not you'll get hired for a particular job. Employers aren't allowed to look at credit scores, but in situations in which you will be asked to handle a drawer of cash, they often look at credit reports for signs of financial trouble. They've learned it's not necessarily a good idea to put a person in front of a drawer of twenties when they have a stack of delinquent bills at home.

It's Not Score—It's Scores

In reality, you have more than one credit score; you have many. The majority of scores are produced by a California-based company named FICO (formerly Fair, Isaac and Company). FICO doesn't collect credit information—it's not a credit bureau—but it works with all three of the large credit bureaus to take the information they collect and turn it into credit, or FICO, scores. Those scores are processed with different criteria in mind for mortgage lenders (who buy them and want to see a score that emphasizes your track record in paying housing–related debts), auto lenders (who do the same, but want to see an emphasis on auto debt) and credit card companies (ditto, with an emphasis on credit card debt). And those are just the scores processed by FICO.

There are more. The three large credit bureaus process—and sell—scores of their own under names like the PLUS Score, from Experian; TrueCredit, from TransUnion; and VantageScore, which, confusingly enough, was developed by the three credit bureaus working together and offers both a score (not, unfortu–nately, on the same scale as the FICO) and a letter grade. And there are other, smaller players in the market as well. If it sounds perplexing, it is. The traditional FICO score looks a lot like your math or verbal SAT score. It ranges from about 350 (though it's rare to see one below 500) to 850 (equally rare). The newfangled scores can go higher (Vantage scores top out at 990). There's also something called an insurance score; we'll get to that in a few pages.

How do you sort through the clutter? By going back

to basics. The score that matters, the score that you want to buy if and when you need one (more on that in a moment), is the one the lender is most likely to see.

That means a version of your FICO score. You can get both your Equifax FICO score and your TransUnion FICO score at myfico.com. (At press time, they were $15.95 each.) You cannot, unfortunately, purchase your Experian FICO; you can purchase only the PLUS. Does it make sense to buy the PLUS? I don't see the logic in it if that's not what your lenders are going to see. But you should still make a point to get your Experian credit report and correct any mistakes that could be dragging your score down.

The most important thing for you to take away from this section is that your score is a really powerful piece of information. And because it is a snapshot of your borrowing and bill-paying behavior over the previous twenty-four months, you have the power to change it for the better as time goes by. As you do that, you'll be able to swap some of your higher-rate credit card debts, mortgages, and auto loans for lower-rate ones, and that will enable you to pay back the money you owe both faster and more cheaply.

So, I want you to check your credit score at the start of this process. You're not going to micromanage it, but

after twelve months—or if you apply for a mortgage—
you're going to check it again to see how you're
doing.

What Can a Good Credit Score Do for You?

When I originally wrote *Pay It Down!*, I noted: "If you
have a credit score of more than 620—and the vast
majority of people do—you will be able to borrow
more money. However, only when you get that score
up past the 700—or even 720—mark will you be able
to borrow that money at the very best prices." Times
have changed. Today you need to be above 660 to be
passable, 700 to be good, and 750 to be great.

Why are these scores so important? Because of something called "risk-based pricing," a relatively new phe-
nomenon in the lending industry. Back in the 1980s,
everyone who had a credit card from Citibank, for example, paid the same rate. But as credit-scoring technol-
ogy improved, it became possible for Citibank to learn
that Jane Doe was more likely to pay her bills on time
than John Doe. So Citi—and the rest of the lenders in
this country—decided that they'd fare better (in other
words, keep their best customers happier *and* make
more money) by rewarding Jane with a lower interest

rate and penalizing Joe with a higher one. After all, Jane, who paid all her bills in full and on time, wasn't paying anything in interest anyway. That's why these days all lenders, not just credit card companies, use some form of risk–based pricing.

The score that you need to get that best price (or at least not the worst one) varies by the product you're shopping for.

Your mortgage and your score. The score you need to qualify for a plain–vanilla thirty–year fixed–rate mort- gage is 620. That qualifies you for a mortgage that Fan- nie Mae and Freddie Mac will purchase in the secondary market. But that 620 isn't going to buy you a very good interest rate. As you'll see in the chart that follows, even small improvements in your score can mean a huge savings in your mortgage. Improving your score by one hundred points from 620 to 720 can mean an extra $90,000 in your pocket over the life of your loan.

Let's say you're borrowing $200,000 to buy a house. Using the January 2004 prime rate of 4 percent, the chart on the opposite page shows you what that loan would cost you—on average—based on your credit score:

Your auto loan and your score. Auto lenders are com- pletely aware that bringing in a customer with a score of, say, 640 is significantly better than bringing in a customer with a score of 600. They have detailed models that tell them that 640 borrowers are *half* as likely to default on their loans. And the prices reflect that: On a $20,000 car loan in January 2004, a customer with a 640 score would have saved $2,000 in interest over the life of a sixty-month loan, as shown in the chart on page 30:

Your credit cards and your score. In general, the credit card industry works the same way: the higher your score, the lower your interest rate. There really is no credit score—not even 500—at which you can't qualify for a credit card. The bank may ask you to deposit some money to secure the credit until you prove (after eighteen

COST OF $200,000 HOUSE LOAN

Score	Interest Rate	Monthly Payment	Total Interest Paid Over 30 Years
720–850	5.501%	$1,136	$208,853
700–719	5.626%	$1,151	$214,518
675–699	6.163%	$1,220	$239,250
620–674	7.313%	$1,373	$294,247
560–619	8.531%	$1,542	$355,200
500–559	9.289%	$1,651	$394,362

COST OF $20,000 CAR LOAN

Score	Interest Rate	Monthly Payment	Total Interest Paid Over 5 Years
720–850	4.931%	$460	$2,078
700–719	5.659%	$467	$2,396
675–699	7.894%	$487	$3,389
620–674	10.808%	$515	$4,722
560–619	15.126%	$558	$6,779
500–559	18.530%	$593	$8,467

or twenty-four months) that you'll pay your bills. But you can still get one.

Interestingly, you can get to the point where a credit card issuer thinks your score is too high. In a credit card issuer's world, a score of 720 or 730 is optimal; 800 is too high. How is that possible? There's a correlation between credit inactivity and a very high score. People who use a credit card rarely or only in case of an emergency represent more of a cost than a benefit to credit card companies. Such people rarely pay their bills late—and they certainly aren't very risky—but card companies still have to send them a statement once a month and still have to send them literature when they make a change in the credit card program. If you're this sort of person, the card company may eventually decide they don't want to do business with you.

How Can You Increase Your Score?

There are a number of ways you can improve your score. For example, while it sounds like a no-brainer, you should be consistent about using your name. Use the same one all the time: first, middle (if you're including one), and last, as well as any Jrs. or IIIs. If you hyphenate, hyphenate with regularity. If you've decided to take your maiden name as your middle name, make it legal. That way, the credit bureaus are less likely to confuse your information with that of someone else. Beyond that, you can improve your score by taking a look at how it is computed—and knowing what you need to do to improve in each area.

Thirty-five percent of your score is based upon how well you pay your bills.

How to boost your score: Start paying on time. If you make late payments, the amount your score will suffer depends on how late and how frequent your delinquencies are. One thirty- or sixty-day late payment is a lot less damaging than fifteen late payments during the past fifteen years. It also matters how recently these episodes occurred. A single incident five months ago still counts. A single incident five years ago no longer matters. For example, one late payment in the recent past could lower your score twenty points. (One that's currently late, and still unpaid, could drop it *double* that.) A pattern of late payments could lower your score fifty or sixty points.

Thirty percent of your score is what FICO calls "balance and burden," a measure of how much credit you have available to you and how much of that credit you're using.

How to boost your score: You're in the best shape if you're using just 10 to 20 percent of the credit available to you. But the way to get to that level is not by canceling and cutting up all your credit cards. I know that's what you've been told to do, but the people telling you that are wrong.

I'm not saying you'll never cancel a credit card. You may decide, as you go through the Pay It Down program, that you need to lighten up on the plastic in your wallet. You just need to understand that in the short term, can–celing cards will have a negative impact on your score.

Why? Think of the percentage of credit you're using now—your credit utilization—as a fraction:

$$\frac{\text{Credit you're using}}{\text{Credit available to you}} = \text{Credit utilization}$$

Say you have ten cards and each of those has a $1,000 limit. You have $10,000 in revolving credit available to you. Now suppose you're using only five of your cards and that those five cards are all maxed out. You're using half of the credit available to you, which puts your credit utilization at 50 percent:

$$\frac{\$5,000}{\$10,000} = 50\%$$

If you decide you don't need all of those cards—that you're going to tidy up your wallet and close the five you're not using—you dramatically reduce the credit you have available to you. Now you're using *all* of the credit you have available, which puts your credit utilization at 100 percent:

$$\frac{\$5,000}{\$5,000} = 100\%$$

This level of utilization could send your score down by a hundred points.

Now, that doesn't mean you should *never* cancel credit cards. If you have been struggling to get out of credit card debt and you've made progress, and you don't want to be tempted to dig yourself back in, then by all means, cancel the cards. You would be sacrificing your score in the short term for much longer-term financial well-being. What you should *not* do, however, is cancel cards right before you apply for a mortgage, auto loan, or other big loan. Instead, use the cards once a month, pay them off when the bill arrives, and during the rest of the month keep them locked away where you won't be tempted to touch them. (You don't want to not use the cards at all—then you run the risk of the card issuer canceling *you*.) Then after you get your mortgage or auto loan, call and cancel. As you make progress paying down the other credit cards in your wallet, your ratio will come back in line and your score will rise.

(*Note:* Don't worry that paying off your balances every month is a bad thing—it isn't. By the time you receive your bill, write your check, and mail it in and it's cashed, posted, and reported to the credit bureaus, you've already gotten the bill for the next month. In other words, if you're making frequent use of your card, you never show a zero balance to the bureaus.)

Ten percent of your score is based on your search for new credit—how recently you have opened (or inquired about opening) new accounts.

How to boost your score: Today, the smart shopper doesn't just walk into the local bank and apply for a mortgage. She shops around for the best rate, going online to see what sorts of deals are available, calling a local mortgage broker, and perhaps applying at that local bank, where they might give her a preferential rate because she's been a good customer for years. Along the way, it wouldn't be unusual for ten or fifteen different institutions to check her credit score. Her score won't be in jeopardy if she shops around in that way. Auto- or mortgage-related inquiries (resulting in a score being pulled by the auto or mortgage lender) that occur within thirty days of each other simply say to the credit bureau that you're shopping for a car or a house, and they're counted as one inquiry.

When a credit card company pulls your report, however, it's another story. A single application for a single card isn't a sign of trouble, but multiple card inquiries are a sign that you need money. Generally, that's not good. Multiple inquiries, particularly if you've had credit for only a few years, can mean a loss of fifty to one hundred points on your score.

(*Note:* This means that when you hit the mall, it's not a good idea to accept every offer for instant credit—even if it means you're going to get 15 percent off the cost of your purchase. I understand the offers are compelling. I also understand that it's been a long time since the salesclerk hasn't asked you if you want to "save 15 percent." I know that some of those salesclerks will even advise you simply to close the account if you don't want it after you get home. Closing the account, however, won't stop the inquiry from damaging your credit rating. So bide your time. Save the 15 percent offer for when you're buying a $2,700 couch, not a $27 handbag.)

Ten percent is the financial composition of your file: What percentage is bank-card debt and what percentage is installment debt?

How to boost your score: In the world of credit scoring, balance is important. It's better to have a ratio of 60:40 or 70:30 bank-card debt to installment debt than to have too much more of one or the other. If your ratios are out of whack, you can use these guidelines to help you pay back one lender or another. But don't obsess over this component. It's the hardest element to control and represents a relatively small portion of your score.

Fifteen percent is based on the length of your credit relationships: How long have you had the cards in your wallet?

How to boost your score: If and when you decide to cancel your credit cards, try not to cancel the ones you've had the longest. It's good to have at least one card in your wallet that's more than two years old. Once you've had a card for fifteen to twenty years, it won't send your score any higher.

You'll be surprised at how quickly the changes you make can boost your score. It's quite possible to see an increase of twenty-five points inside of a year, according to the folks at FICO.

When might you *not* see that kind of a boost? Increasing your score will be more difficult if you have a bankruptcy in your history or more than one ninety-day late payment. At that point, you're going to have to keep your behavior in check for the next couple of years while simultaneously following the foregoing advice. In other words, *wait it out.* Your score can improve as negative information moves toward the back—or, better yet, falls off your report. Credit scores are built to *predict* what will happen over the next twenty-four months: how likely it is that you'll fall behind in your payments over that time period. For that reason, it makes the most sense, analytically, to the lender to weigh most heavily your behavior over the *previous* twenty-four months. So negative information counts less after it's more than twenty-four months old. Unfortunately, even if you've cleaned up bad behavior, it takes time for negative information to vanish completely. Although some states have legislated this on their own—in New York, for example, negative information can stay on your report only five years—most of the country sticks to this schedule:

- Late payments: seven years
- Debt-management plan (through credit counselor): seven years
- Bankruptcy: ten years

What should you do with all of this information? Use it to guide your behavior over the next twelve months and beyond. Of course, you're not going to wait until your credit score has improved to start putting aside your $10 a day and using it to your advantage. But as your scores improve, you'll be able to manage your interest rates, as well, swapping your high-rate cards for lower-rate ones. As I said, that's a few months down the road. Right now, it's time to come up with some cash.

Your Insurance Score Is a Little Different

As I noted before, auto- and homeowners-insurance companies (sometimes called property-casualty insurers) often use what's called an insurance score to help them determine how risky a proposition you are for them. This is information that plays into how much you'll pay in premiums and your eligibility for coverage (though it's typically not the deciding factor). An insurance score, though, is different from the standard credit score that your credit card company or mortgage lender uses. To begin with, it's tabulated by a different company, ChoicePoint.

ChoicePoint pulls together your prior-claim history and your credit history to develop your magic number, which is marketed to insurers and to you as a Choice-Point Attract Insurance Score. As with your credit score, it comes with a detailed report, which in this case is called a C.L.U.E., or Comprehensive Loss Underwriting Exchange report. There are separate scores and reports for auto and home insurance.

Why go to all the trouble? Insurance companies have conducted study after study proving that customers with low credit scores file more insurance claims. They believe that your credit score is a better indicator of how much money you'll cost them over time than even your driving record. And because insurance companies need to make money, they shy away from extending coverage to people who have historically filed a lot of claims, or people who they believe will file a lot of claims in the future. (Or they simply charge these people significantly more for the coverage.) Both of these things are reflected in your C.L.U.E. report and your Attract auto– and home–insurance scores.

Keep in mind, though, that this number represents only a portion of what goes into determining your eligibility for coverage and the amount you'll pay for premiums. Companies combine the score with the other underwriting guidelines they use—your driving record with your state, or your claim history as a homeowner—to ultimately evaluate your risk.

Confusing matters, naturally, is the fact that Choice-Point's Attract scores don't operate on the same scale as FICO scores. They go up to 997, and the higher you fall on that scale, the better. Here's how they break it down:

Score	Ranking
776–997	Good
626–775	Average
501–625	Below Average
Under 500	Less Desirable

As with your credit reports from the three major credit bureaus, you're entitled to a free copy of your C.L.U.E. report once a year. You can get it by going to choicetrust.com (ChoiceTrust is a division of Choice-Point), clicking on the C.L.U.E. Reports link, and clicking the link to order your FACT Act Disclosure. You can also request it by mail or phone:

C.L.U.E. Inc. Consumer Disclosure Center
Attn: FACT Act Request
P.O. Box 105295
Atlanta, GA 30348
866-312-8076

As far as your Attract score, you have to pay for it, just like your credit score. Each score—home and auto—is $12.95, and it comes with a copy of your Equifax credit report.

Tales of Life and Debt:
Recovering from a Lousy Credit Score, Dollar by Dollar

Several years ago, Lydia and Brian, a two–career couple in Washington, D.C., decided they wanted to build a house. They found a builder they wanted to work with and a subdivision in suburban Maryland in which they wanted to live, and, excited at the prospects, went about prequalifying for a mortgage. All of a sudden, their bubble burst.

Mortgage rates at the time were at near–historic lows. Lydia and Brian were counting on using those rates to help them build a house big enough to grow into. But their potential lender told them they would be able to qualify only for rates two to three percentage points higher. Why? Lousy credit scores.

"We knew we had six to nine months before the home was ready—we were building from the ground up," explains Lydia. "So we decided to take the time to work on improving our credit scores and our overall financial situation."

The first thing they needed to know was what, precisely, was dragging their scores down. They pulled both their credit scores and their credit reports. Without too much detective work, they found the culprits. "One reason our credit scores were so low was that there was a lot of outdated information on our credit reports," Lydia explains. Accounts had been closed. Late payments that had occurred more than seven years earlier should have already dropped off the report. Lydia and Brian took matters into their own hands, sending certified letters to all three credit bureaus disputing the information and noting, specifically, which items should be updated and which should be removed. "It took us some time to clean up those credit reports," Lydia recalls. "I also called or wrote to the various creditors to make sure they updated their records."

The other reason for the couple's low scores was hidden in their bulging wallets: twelve credit cards, each used to 50 percent of its limit or more. That made the couple's debt-to-income ratio—an important component of their credit scores—higher than it should have been. No amount of letter writing, even certified letter writing, could take care of that. Instead, Lydia and Brian had to hunker down.

They decided to forgo eating out as much as possible. They cut back the money they were spending on clothing and travel. They began to dump every available penny into a money-market account, which they then used to pay off their credit cards. Over the next nine months, they paid off eleven of twelve credit cards—and, to eliminate temptation, closed seven of them. They then stopped using credit cards completely and saved an additional $10,000 to put down on their home.

When they went back to their lender several weeks before they finally closed on the house, he was astonished to see the difference in their credit scores. They had jumped to between 650 and 730 points. The result: Lydia and Brian qualified for a three-year adjustable-rate mortgage at 4.95 percent. With their old scores the rate could have gone as high as 7 percent; their nine-month exercise in frugality saved them $400 a month on their mortgage payment—nearly $5,000 a year.

To this day, Lydia and Brian pull their credit scores every six months to make sure they've remained high, an exercise that has continued to pay off. Just about a year after they started their quest, they refinanced their mortgage at a low and competitive fixed rate for thirty years. "I am an example of a person who learned how to repay her debts," says Lydia, proud of her achievements. It wasn't easy, but she did it—step by step, dollar by dollar. Without professional help.

STEP 4

Track Your Spending

⁓

Ten dollars a day. It sounds like nothing, right? Until you have to come up with it every day without fail. Then it can be a challenge—not insurmountable, mind you, but an activity that requires some thought.

It also requires—and though this may sound like a no-brainer, for many people it's anything but—that you know where your money is going. Most people don't. In fact, many people also don't fully comprehend the fact that they're spending more than they bring in each month. For my book *The Ten Commandments of Financial Happiness*, I worked with the polling folks at RoperASW on a big piece of research. From it we learned that:

- Eighty-five percent of people believe that no matter how much or how little money they make, they'll be able to live on it.
- Half of those people don't pay off their credit card bills each month.
- Half of those people don't save anything.

What does that mean? To me, it means that we've forgotten what it means to live on what we make. By not paying off our credit cards, we're living on borrowed money. By not saving, we're living on borrowed time.

It was very, very different in our parents' day. Their generation was hardwired to save 10 percent of whatever they earned for a rainy day. If and when they had an emergency—whether it was a small one (the transmission dying) or a big one (a health scare)—they were able to draw on that savings. They didn't have to worry (at least for a little while) that they'd lose their homes or fall deep into debt.

But we don't have that kind of safety net. Our national savings rate peaked shortly after the Great Depression, in the 1940s. It tapered off in the fifties and sixties, but by the mid-1980s we were still saving nearly 11 percent of every dollar we made. By 2005, we were spending more than we made—the savings rate was a negative: –2.7 percent.

What happened? Incomes stagnated while prices continued to rise, for one thing. Borrowed money became way too easy to come by, for another.

In the past eighteen months that scenario has reversed itself. As the credit crunch took hold, home equity started to shrink and once-prevalent Home Equity Lines of Credit (or HELOCs) that accompanied it vanished. Fat credit card limits went the same way. So did cash-out mortgage refis. Out went the ability to spend like it was going out of style. In came newfound worry. The silver lining? We started to save. The savings rate during this recession left the negative territory, climbed to 1 percent, 2 percent, 4 percent, and is continuing to climb as I write this.

Now, it's important to note that in other recent recessions the savings rate has spiked as well—and the change has been way too temporary. As soon as the job numbers stopped falling and Americans felt secure once again, the savings rate reverted to its anemic state. Is this time different for America? I believe the answer is yes, that the downturn has been deep and devastating enough that the improved savings rate will stick. But even if it's not for America, it can be for *you*.

Fixing Your Own Financial House

Here's the lowdown: We may earn a decent living in this country—in many families we earn two—but we spend as much as we earn on our mortgages, car loans, day care, and other "fixed" expenses. When an emergency hits, we don't have the savings our parents had to draw on. If we lose a job, as so many have recently, or suffer an illness or have to take a break from the workforce to care for a child who's having trouble in school or a parent who's getting on in years, our finances simply can't handle it. You hear people time and time again talking about the "fragile middle class." This lack of a safety net—of savings—is what makes us so fragile.

How do we turn the situation around? The *only* way to do it is to start living within our means and saving a little something in good times and in bad, just in case. The only way to do that is to know:

• What's coming in
• What's going out
• Where it's going

What's Coming In

Do you know how much money you'll earn this year—before *and* after taxes? That after-tax number is the key. Mentally budgeting to live on your gross, or pretax, income is a guarantee that you'll overspend. Say you're a single person earning a gross salary of $48,000 a year, a very decent number. If you plan on spending anywhere near that $48,000, you've overdone it, because even if you live in a state that doesn't raid the pot, Uncle Sam is going to take an $8,188 cut. And you'll end up $8,188 in the hole.

So stop and take a look at how much you're bringing in before and after taxes. Use the chart on page 50 to record your information. If you receive a regular paycheck, this information is on your pay stub. If you work for yourself and business has been pretty consistent, then use last year's earnings as a guide. Use last year's number even if you think you're going to earn more this year; being conservative is insurance that you won't spend more than you actually bring in. Write down your earnings number. Apply your tax rate. The resulting difference is what you're working with. Divide this by twelve. That's your monthly take-home pay.

Your annual pretax income: $_____

Your annual after–tax income: $_____

Your monthly after–tax income: $_____

What's Going Out

You have two different types of expenses: fixed and variable. Your fixed costs represent the money you've already agreed to spend each month. Think of them as things you need, things that are nonnegotiable and indispensable. (In reality, many of them are likely *very* negotiable and *quite* dispensable. We'll come back to that in a minute.)

The chart that follows includes items that you pay quarterly or semiannually, such as home and auto insurance. In recording your expenses, divide your payments into monthly increments to get an accurate assessment of what it's costing you each month. And since we're dealing with fixed costs, use just the minimum you're required to pay each month on your credit cards here.

Your fixed expenses

Rent/mortgage $_____

Common charges (condo fees, etc.) $_____

Car payment 1 $_____

Car payment 2 $_____

Car payment 3 $_____

Train ticket or other
   commuting expenses $_____

Child support $_____

Alimony $_____

Back taxes $_____

Parking expenses $_____

Student-loan payment $_____

Credit card payment $_____

Electric $_____

Gas $_____

Oil $_____

Water $_____

Other utilities $_____

Health club $_____

Internet $_____

Phone (landline) $_____

Wireless (phone/PDA) $_____

Cable $_____

Child care/babysitter $_____

Health insurance $_____

Homeowners insurance $_____

Auto insurance $_____

Life insurance $_____

Regular prescriptions $_____

Payments for other purchases
    (furniture, appliances, etc.) $_____

Housekeeper $_____

Lawn care $_____

College tuition $_____

Private school $_____

Tutoring $_____

After-school programs $_____

Sports for the kids $_____

Summer camp $_____

Other $_____

Fixed expenses monthly total   **$_____**

Once you add up the numbers, you'll be able to see the difference between what you make each month and what you've *already agreed* to spend each month. If you're surprisingly close to the line—or over it—you're not the only one. For many, many people (particularly those who've overborrowed or who live in big cities), housing alone eats up 50 percent of what they take home each month. That immediately sets them up to fail. But although you may perceive these expenses to be "fixed," they're not, really. There are ways that you can cut almost every one. But before you do that, you need to know how much you're spending in areas that aren't fixed as well.

Where's the Rest of Your Money Going?

Even if you have some wiggle room in the fixed categories, you may still feel like you're strangled with debt and unable to save. That may be because you're spending too much on other things.

I'll bet, however, that if I asked you how much you spend on these variable items, you'd have absolutely no idea. That's because the amounts vary from month to month. It's also because few of us keep track of where our cash goes. We head to the ATM, withdraw $50 or $100, spend it randomly, and withdraw another chunk of cash when the money's gone. Keeping track is too time consuming, too detail oriented, so most of us simply don't bother. But while you're going through this makeover, you have to bother. The only way to get a realistic idea of what you're spending your money on is to track it.

So, I want you to get a little notebook, one small enough to fit in your pocket or your purse. Slide a pen through the spirals so there will be no "but I didn't have a pen" excuses for not writing things down. Starting today, I want you to write down everything you spend. *Everything.* You may not think it matters that you drop 75 cents a day into the vending machine at work, but that

75 cents is $16.25 a month and $195 a year. In other words, it's a plane ticket, part of a car payment—*it's real money*.

When you get home each night, categorize those expenses on a legal pad. For a month, keep running totals of how much you're spending on:

Your variable expenses

Groceries	$_____
Restaurant meals	$_____
Take-out breakfast	$_____
Take-out lunch	$_____
Take-out dinner	$_____
Coffee	$_____
Snacks	$_____
Gasoline	$_____
Clothing, shoes, accessories	$_____
Entertaining (dinner parties, cocktail parties)	$_____
Entertainment (movies, theater tickets, sporting events)	$_____

Dry cleaning $_____

Cards $_____

Gifts (and gift wrap) $_____

Newspapers and magazines $_____

Books $_____

CDs/music $_____

Videos/DVDs $_____

Things for the house
   (sheets, towels, kitchen
   accessories, decorating) $_____

Wine, beer, liquor $_____

Cigarettes $_____

Drugstore expenses
   (shampoo, nonprescription
   medications) $_____

Other medical expenses
   (appointments, services that
   aren't reimbursed) $_____

Grooming expenses
   (manicures, haircuts) $_____

Pet food $_____

Pet grooming $_____

Veterinary bills $_____

Other $_____

**Variable expenses
    monthly total** $_____

Okay, so now it's time to see where you stand. First, get a total of how much you're spending each month:

Monthly total fixed expenses $_____

\+ Monthly total variable expenses $_____

= Monthly total expenses $_____

Now, let's see whether you're exceeding your income.

Monthly after-tax income $_____

– Monthly total expenses $_____

**= Your monthly profit
    (savings) or loss** $_____

How'd you do? When you add together your fixed and variable expenses and then subtract them from your after-tax income, are you still in positive territory? If you are, then you are essentially living on what you make. That doesn't mean there's no room for improvement; by spending less, you can save more and pay down your existing debts faster. That will mean more money in your pocket and less padding of your credit card companies' accounts— and that will help you get a lock on your financial future.

If you're not in positive territory—or if you're so close there's no wiggle room—you're spending too much. It's time to turn that equation around and get yourself out of the red, into the black, and on the road to personal profitability.

Tales of Life and Debt:
"We Didn't Know How Much We Spent!"

"I wasn't very well educated in the world of money," says Al, a project manager for a telecommunications company in Atlanta. "And that made it one of the most difficult topics for me to talk about. I never asked my parents how much they made. They never sat me down to go over what a budget is. One day after I graduated from college and started making money and spending money, my father sat me down and asked where my money was going. I said, 'Hey, Dad. Did you earn this money? No. Then don't ask me.'"

Al probably would have been better off if he'd had that conversation with his father no matter how uncomfortable it made him. As it was, it took him a good decade to figure out precisely where his money was going—and that decade sabotaged his ability to save as much as possible for everything from college tuition to retirement.

Al and his wife, Jean, have been married for twenty years. At the beginning of their life together, he went to work and she handled the at-home budgeting—a very traditional division of labor. But over the years, Al realized that although he knew how much he was bringing home in each paycheck (and roughly how much Jean was taking in from her part-time job), he had very little idea where they were spending all that money.

That was just the beginning of their downward spiral. Although neither Al nor his wife was raised with credit cards, both developed an affinity for charging. They convinced themselves they were spending money on things they needed. Al would walk into a department store and blow $1,400 on four suits he needed for work. Together, they wouldn't think twice about charging a $150 dinner on a weekend, then spending another $30 at the movies.

They lived this sort of free-spending life for years. Then one day they realized that the balances on their combined cards had hit $20,000. They had no money in the bank and no retirement savings to speak of. Jean panicked. "She was worrying continuously for about six months," Al said. He took a step back and decided panicking wasn't going to do them any good. "I said, 'This is crazy. We just have to stop charging. We need to put the cards away and be disciplined.'"

The next week he picked up a copy of Quicken, the popular personal-finance software. Quicken—though it does many other, more sophisticated, tasks as well—is, at its core, an electronic check register. You input how much you spend on which specific items; it deducts the expenditures from your overall balance. Whenever you'd like to know how much you're spending by category, you can simply push a button and see your spending habits in pie-chart form.

Al was amazed. "When you're just looking at the individual numbers, the individual expenses, you really have no idea what you're spending your money on. I was amazed at how much we spent on groceries; how much we spent on our cars. When you're just looking at your balance, you're not thinking ahead about where you want your money to go." But that's what Quicken forced him to do—to start choosing where his money might do him the most good.

And over the past few years, making those choices has enabled Al and Jean to dig their way out of debt. They stopped eating out as frequently; stopped spending money on cars and clothes. It took two and a half years for them to clear the $20,000 in credit card debt. But they didn't stop there. They started overpaying on their car loan, tacking on another $150 to the $350 they owed each month. The result: They shaved a year and a half off the term of the loan. They're overpaying on their mortgage, as well, aiming to have the house paid in full in the next five years. The credit cards in their lives have been replaced by debit cards—although they have continued to hold off on big expenses. (Al would like a new car to replace his second one, a nine-year-old Honda, but he says, "I just don't want to cut the check for a new car. I want to write a check to the mutual fund for that amount.") And they're saving. "We still don't have a full three months' emergency savings," Al acknowledges. "But we have something."

Al sums it up: "By the time I'm fifty, I want to know that my house is paid off. I want to know I have money in the bank. I don't want the stress of owing money to other people. I want my balance sheet to be absolutely clean."

STEP 5

Find the Money

———

Did you ever see the movie *Dave?* In it, Kevin Kline played a look-alike for the president of the United States who takes over the job when the real president has a stroke while fooling around with his secretary. (Yes, it's a comedy.) In one scene Dave is faced with shutting down a day-care center for underprivileged kids—unless he can find some wiggle room in the government's budget. So he brings his hometown CPA (Charles Grodin) to the White House and they sit around the kitchen table at midnight, chowing down and figuring out where they can make cuts. They get creative. And they succeed.

And that's precisely what you need to do.

Before we dive in, though, you need to agree that you'll be willing to make some hard choices about spending money on particular items. Let's take your cell phone as an example. If you're like many people, you've come to rely very heavily on your cell phone. You may have started out using it for convenience, or only in emergencies, but over the last few years, it's become the easiest and best way to reach you. You can't imagine giving it up. Or can you? Analysts say the average cell-phone bill is $50 a month. That's $600 a year. Could you give it up—or use it substantially less often—if that was what you needed to do to come up with your $10 a day? How about your multiple movie channels? Or the health club you rarely use? Or your second car? Or that second dinner out each week?

These are hard questions. And no one can answer them for you. The problem is that if you're not balancing your budget already, you may not be able to do it by getting rid of the small expenditures (the example that seems to come up most often is the latte, but maybe for you it's taxi fare or magazines at the supermarket checkout). You may have to eliminate or trim some bigger line items.

I'll make you a deal: I'll go through this process in an order designed to cause you the least pain, one that will ask you to give up the fewest things in life that you enjoy. But once you've found your $10 a day, it's up to you: You can stop reading, knowing that you've succeeded (and it's a success that should be celebrated!), or you can continue and determine if there's a way for you to build a savings cushion more quickly, or a larger nest egg. Or you can use the excess to save for other goals you might have in mind.

For example:

What could you do with an extra $50 a month?
    Replace your decrepit dishwasher
    Join a gym

What could you do with an extra $100 a month?
    Buy season tickets to your favorite sports team's games
    Take your family on a four-day vacation

What could you do with an extra $200 a month?
    Pay for your newborn child's future wedding
    Send your teenager to sleepaway camp for a month

What could you do with an extra $500 a month?
    Put a two-year-old through college in sixteen years
    Put a down payment on a home in five years

So let's go through the process. At the end of each step, I want you to keep a running total of how much money you were able to find.

Find the Money: Change Your Withholding

Did you get a tax refund last year? Do you seem to get one every year? You may love the thought of getting a nice fat check to brighten up each winter, but you should *not* be giving Uncle Sam an interest-free loan in the first place. (If the shoe were on the other foot, the government wouldn't give one to you.) Plus, the money would serve you better if you were getting it in consistent pieces throughout the year.

How much would changing your withholding put in *your* pocket?

Found Money: $_____/month

(You'll find these total lines throughout the book. Use them to keep track of how much you're able to free up each month. And don't worry, there are a lot of these blanks to come. You'll find that even small amounts can quickly add up.)

Find the Money: Reduce Your Interest Rates

When you take a look at the expenses listed in the previous section, you'll notice many of them are borrowing costs:

- Mortgage
- Home equity loan or line of credit
- Car loan
- Student loan
- Credit card payments

From the late 1990s through the first part of the twenty-first century, we've been fortunate to enjoy some of the lowest interest rates in history. About half of Americans used these low borrowing costs to their advantage. They strengthened their balance sheets by refinancing their mortgages (and banking the cash), paying off their credit cards at teaser rates, and paying off their student loans ahead of schedule. The other half—including, I'll bet, many of you reading this book—used the low interest rates and the increased willingness of all types of lenders to dole out money to borrow more, and more, and more. That half bought new cars with new car loans before paying off their old ones. That half drained the equity from their mortgages with cash-out refis or home equity lines of credit to pay off fat credit card balances and then charged those credit cards right back up again. I suspected we were headed for trouble. That was why I wrote this book in 2004. Even I had no idea how deep or devastating the trouble would prove to be.

In short order, housing prices stalled. Interest rates popped. Credit dried up. Stocks cratered. Bottom line: We had no way to get the money we needed to service our debts. We couldn't get it from our fat stock portfolios because they were diminished. We couldn't pull it out of our mortgages because, even if the houses were still worth more than we owed on them—and so many were not—the lenders weren't willing to lend.

It took intervention from the government to get things moving again. And by mid-2009, though things were far from perfect, housing prices looked headed for a bottom, the stock market had come roaring back (whether or not it would stick is still anybody's guess), and most important, interest rates were once again historically low.

What that means is that many, many Americans get a mulligan. If you weren't among the faction that used low interest rates to their advantage—to improve their balance sheets—the first time around, then you have a chance to do it again.

Don't blow it.

Find the Money: Cut Your Credit Card Interest

Cutting your credit card interest rate isn't, unfortunately, as easy as it used to be. Until 2009, I felt very comfortable telling consumers looking for a lower interest rate from their credit card companies simply to call those card companies and ask. Research had shown that about 50 percent of the time the simple phone-call method worked. The other 50 percent of the time, it didn't. No big deal. You weren't any worse off than you were before.

No more. Beginning in about March 2009, I was hearing anecdotal report after anecdotal report of consumers who were calling their credit card companies to request that lower interest rate and were told that their rates were going up instead. Or that their credit limits were being cut.

This seemed astonishing—so I did some digging. According to sources within the industry, the phone call itself wasn't triggering the higher rate or the slashed credit line. The industry insisted that had been happening behind the scenes and consumers simply happened to phone their card companies before they received the letter of notification in the mail. I could buy that. But what also seemed to be happening on those phone calls was that the customer–service reps on the other end of the line were being told to ask for the sort of information that wouldn't show up on a customer's credit report. If they asked questions about layoffs, salary reductions, and furloughs and were given information that indicated a customer's situation had changed for the worse, they could use it to augment their case for increasing interest rates or cutting credit limits.

Thankfully, Congress has interceded. The Credit CARD Act—more commonly called the Credit Cardholders' Bill of Rights—passed the Senate and the House on consecutive days in May 2009, and later that same weekend President Obama signed it into law. It includes the following changes:

The Credit Cardholders' Bill of Rights

- **First Year of New Card.** Credit card issuers may not raise interest rates in the first year after a card is issued except: At the end of a promotional (teaser) rate of at least six months. If the card is a variable–interest–rate card. If the minimum payment is not received within sixty days after the due date.

- **Interest Rates on Existing Balances.** Interest rates on existing balances cannot be increased unless: A card is a variable-interest-rate card. A promotional rate has come to an end. The minimum payment is not received within sixty days after the due date.

- **Changing the Terms.** Card companies can't change the terms for repaying old balances, except the issuer may give you: Five years to pay off the outstanding balance at the old rate, or a new minimum payment that is no more than twice the old one.

- **Interest-Rate Increases.** Card companies must give consumers at least forty-five days' notice before raising the interest rate on future purchases (unless a rate increase is due to an increase in a variable rate or the expiration of a promotional rate).

- **Changes in Payments.** When a card has several different interest rates (balance transfers, cash advances, purchases), payment must be applied to the highest interest rate first. Bills must be delivered at least twenty-one days before the due date. Payment can be received up until five p.m. on the due date without being considered late.

- **Cards for People Under Twenty-one.** Card issuers can no longer provide gifts on campus for students who fill out card applications. To receive a card, anyone under twenty-one must have a cosigner over age twenty-one or prove that they have income to support repayment.

continued

- **Changes in Penalties/Fees.**
  - Interest rates that go up because of sixty-day late payment must go back to their original lower rates after six months of on-time payments.
  - Consumers must opt in to be allowed to exceed their credit limit. If they do opt in and exceed, they will be charged only one over-limit fee per billing cycle.
  - No fees can be charged to make a payment except when expedited through a service rep.

So what's the solution today to bring down the credit card interest rates you already have? First, you need to know where you stand. Start by laying all your cards out on the table and listing the APR (annual percentage rate, or interest rate) you're paying on each. Note whether those rates are fixed or variable. You'll also want to have a rough idea of how valuable a customer you've been: how you've had the card, how much you charge a month or year, how much interest they're earning each year on your business, and whether you pay on time.

Next, ready your ammunition. The preapproved offers you've received in the mail are no guarantee that you'll actually get those rates, but a steady stream of offers is a good indication that you're a valuable customer to have. When you've got it together, you can proceed. Knowing what your credit score is and whether it's good, bad, or somewhere in the middle is important too.

There are two instances in which calling your card company is still a good idea:

If you're too valuable to lose. If you have a good credit score, if you are an active customer (i.e., you spend a lot of money on the card or don't pay it off in full every month), and *if you have offers to go elsewhere,* pick up the phone and call your card company. Then follow—and do not deviate from—this script. I don't want you giving your card company information that they can use against you.

> *"I have [name of card] with you and my interest rate is [X] percent. I received another offer in the mail from [other bank's name] for [X] percent, but before I take it, I want to see if you can lower my interest rate instead."*

If the representative says they're not authorized to do that, you say:

> *"Look, you and I both know that if I transfer my balance today, next week your bank is going to send me an offer to*

*come back at an even lower rate. Why don't you just save
the bank the cost of that effort by giving me several points
today?"*

If the rep says it's not possible because your credit
card is at a fixed interest rate, you say:

*"Actually, that doesn't have anything to do with whether
or not you have the ability to lower my interest rate. A
fixed interest rate only means that my rate doesn't vary
with fluctuations in the prime rate. In fact, the bank can
raise it on new purchases on my account at any time by
just giving me forty-five days' written notice. And the
bank can—if it chooses—lower the rate today."*

If the rep still says they're not authorized to do that,
you say:

"I'd like to speak to your supervisor."

• *Speak to a supervisor and ask again.* Even if you get a
substantial cut in the interest rate from the first person, it's worth speaking to a supervisor to see if you
can do any better. The person on the front line of customer service will be authorized only to cut your rate
by a preset amount (if at all). The customer-service
representative may also insist that the supervisor

doesn't have the power to cut your rate either, or if you've already gotten a break, to cut it further. That may not be true, so insist on speaking to the supervisor anyway.

• *Threaten to close your account.* Let me be clear here: You don't *want* to close your account. It won't do good things to your credit score. However, if the bank believes that you're willing to close your account, and if you've been a profitable customer, then you stand a better chance of getting what you want.

• *Keep a record of whom you spoke to and what was said.* If your promised rate cut—or fee waiver—doesn't materialize, then you're going to need a paper trail to back up your story. Knowing to whom you spoke, when the call was placed, and what was promised is key.

• *Transfer your balance.* If you're not successful in reducing your interest rate over the phone, it's time to transfer your balance. There are two places to find good balance-transfer offers: your mailbox and Web sites, including bankrate.com and cardweb.com.

Once you've decided to transfer your balance to another card, be sure to consider the following:

• *The rate.* Balance-transfer offers often come with teaser rates—i.e., low rates for the first six or twelve months that then shoot sky-high. You're going to be paying off your highest-rate debts first (more about that in Step 9, Pay It Down—Intelligently), but that really means the teaser puts the brakes on the new interest you're accruing on that preexisting debt. For that reason, the rate *after* the teaser expires is just as important (if not more so) than the teaser itself.

• *The fine print.* Balance transfers often incur interest rates different from those for new purchases. Cash advances sometimes have a third rate. It's important to understand at the outset what all of those rates are. It's also important to understand what "preapproved" does and doesn't mean. You may get an offer in the mail that says you're preapproved for a particular card, but while the interest rate in large print looks tempting, you must keep reading. The rest of the text will likely alert you to the fact that the company is using tiered pricing. This means it offers a range of interest rates—from the lowest of the low to the highest of the high—and you will be assigned an APR based on your credit history. The bottom line: You may not be getting the deal you think you are.

• *The fees.* Some card issuers charge a fee for balance transfers. Generally it's a percentage—sometimes capped—of the amount you're moving. The key is to know how much that will cost you before you make your move.

The other time to call your credit card companies to ask for an interest-rate reduction? When you can't pay your bills. If you are having trouble making even your minimum payments each month, then call your card companies and talk to them about a different sort of payment plan—one for a borrower in distress. These come in two forms:

• *Payment plans.* Card companies are cutting deals with their borrowers in which they reduce your interest rate—sometimes to as low as zero—and negotiate a payment you can actually handle to pay off the card, typically in three to five years. You will need to explain why you're in this situation—lost job, medical condition, etc.—and may be asked to provide proof. Your card company will cut off your credit, so you won't be able to use the card anymore. And you should understand that any money the card company agrees to forgo can be considered income on which you have to pay taxes. But you can save thousands if not tens of thousands in interest overall.

• *Negotiated settlements.* The other sort of deal to cut is a negotiated settlement. In this scenario, you call the company—typically after you've been delinquent—and offer to pay a lump-sum percentage of what you owe today to close your account. If the card company is willing to accept your offer, insist that it report to your credit bureaus that your account was paid in full, and then get confirmation of that agreement in writing. That way you'll have it to send to the credit bureaus yourself if the card company does not follow through, and the account should not appear as a negative mark on your credit report.

Heads up! Now that you've worked so hard to reduce your credit card interest rate, you need to know that there's only one way to keep it down: **Pay on time.** Late-payment fees have soared to an average $35 a pop, but more than that, paying more than sixty days late under the new laws can trigger an interest-rate hike—and there is no limit to how high that rate can go. One way to make sure your payments arrive on time is to switch to online bill payment. You can schedule a payment sizable enough to cover your minimum in advance and know without a doubt that your money will get there on time.

Found Money: $_____/month

How to Compare Credit Card Offers

If you've been offered one credit card, you've been offered a dozen. How do you know which one to take? The key is in the box—the Schumer Box, that is. Every credit card solicitation now has to have a disclosure chart (called a Schumer Box after New York senator Charles Schumer, who pushed for it). Line up your offers side by side and compare the following information that each box includes:

- The actual APR (after the introductory/teaser period; the lower the better)
- The formula for computing a variable APR
- The length of the grace period (the longer the better; look for twenty-five days or more)
- The annual fee (many cards these days, except for mileage and platinum cards, don't have one)
- The minimum finance charge
- The transaction fees (for cash advances, balance transfers, etc.)
- The method used for computing your balance ("adjusted balance" which is rare, is best for consumers because any payments you made during the billing period are subtracted; "average daily balance," a good second choice for consumers, is the most common; "two-cycle balance" is against the law under the 2009 credit card reforms)
- The fees charged for paying late and exceeding your credit limit

Find the Money: Refinance Your Car Loan

Not everyone knows this, but you *can* refinance your car loan. In fact, it's much easier than refinancing your mortgage. Why? There is no appraisal process, for one thing. The fees, if any, are minimal. (You may have to pay $5 to $10 to your state's department of motor vehicles to get a new car title.)

Can you benefit?

- Yes, if you didn't shop well in the first place. If you financed through a dealer within the last few years (and have decent credit), you likely got a rate in the 8-to-10-percent range. You can do better.
- Yes, if you still owe a sizable amount. Most lenders require a car to be less than five years old and have a minimum balance of $7,500 in order to refinance.
- Yes, if you're not "upside down" (owing more than your car is worth). Your car is collateral, so many lenders won't underwrite a car that's not worth the amount you owe on the loan.
- Yes, if your credit has improved. If you bought the car when your credit was blemished (or when you had little credit history at all) and you've cleaned up your act, refinancing can mean a significant drop in rates.

So what do you do next?

First, know what your car is worth. You can pull a value out of the Kelley Blue Book on the Web at kbb.com. As long as your car is worth more than you owe, you're in good shape. If not, promise yourself you won't unload this car until you've righted this equation—or, better yet, have paid it off entirely.

Second, shop around. The best car-loan deals typically come from online lenders and credit unions. To find the best rates, head to bankrate.com, where a nifty search engine can pinpoint the best rates nationally and in your area. If you belong to a credit union, call them as well. If you don't belong to a credit union but would like to join (a good idea, as credit unions often have the best savings rates as well as the lowest lending rates), go to cuna.org (the Web site of the Credit Union National Association) for a list of institutions that might be willing to accept you as a member.

Third, apply for a new loan. When you find what you think is the best rate for you, don't hesitate—just go for it. There's very little downside to this. The one thing you *don't* want to do is extend the term of your loan. If you do this and then decide you want out before you're done paying it off, you run the risk of being upside down. That's how you dig into a deeper debt hole. Most lenders will happily match the term that remains on your loan, even if it's between their normal terms of thirty-six, forty-eight, and sixty months.

Fourth, reap the savings. Take a $25,000, forty-eight-month car loan, for example:

Original interest rate: 8 percent
Original monthly payment: $622
New interest rate: 5.4 percent
New monthly payment: $580
Monthly savings: $42
Total savings: $2,016

Found Money: $_____/month

Find the Money: Consolidate Your Student Loans

A few years ago consolidating student loans was all the rage, because nearly everyone had variable-rate loans, meaning the rates were adjusted once a year. When that variable rate dipped lower than it had been in years, borrowers rushed to consolidate and lock in that rate for the life of the loan.

Now all federal loans that originated after July 1, 2006, are fixed-rate loans, meaning the interest will stay at 6.8 percent for the life of the loan. That means that consolidating these isn't necessary—in fact, doing so will actually increase your interest rate by .075 percent. Not much, but certainly something.

If, on the other hand, you happen to have federal loans that originated prior to July 2006 and you haven't consolidated, you may very well want to do so, provided the interest rate you'll receive is lower than the one you have now. Look for a consolidator that provides a couple of perks for doing the deal. The first is an automatic reduction in your interest rate for electing to have your payments electronically drafted out of your checking account. It should be one quarter of 1 percent. The second is a later reduction in your interest rate—typically a full percentage point or two—for making twenty-four, thirty-six, or forty-eight payments on time. Since you can assure your timeliness with those aforementioned electronic payments, this is a no-brainer.

But note that although consolidating is a great move for some borrowers with older loans, it's not the best for all borrowers. If you have an older loan and you've qualified for discounts on your rate by making twenty-four or forty-eight on-time payments, consolidating may mean swapping back to a higher rate. Also, holders of Perkins loans should be wary. Check with your lender to see if by consolidating you'll lose the chance to put your loan on hold for a while (or to have the government pay the interest) if you take certain public-sector jobs or go back to school.

As far as other rules go, there really aren't many. Some lenders will require a minimum balance of $5,000 to consolidate. Students and parents can consolidate education loans, although they must do it separately. Same goes if you're married—you can't consolidate

A Brief Guide to Federal-Loan-Repayment Plans

Standard: You pay a fixed monthly amount for up to ten years.

Extended: Allows you to stretch out the loan term to anywhere from twelve to thirty years, depending on your loan amount. You'll pay less each month but more overall because of interest. This is available only for loans greater than $30,000.

Graduated: You'll start off with a lower monthly payment, which will gradually increase every two years. The term is twelve to thirty years, and the monthly payment must be at least $25 or the amount of accrued interest each month, whichever is greater. The idea here is that as time goes on, you'll earn a higher salary.

your loans with your spouse's. Student loans may be consolidated during the grace period or in repayment, but parent loans can be consolidated at any time.

So why consolidate if you can't lower your interest rate? To reduce your monthly payments. If you're feeling so squeezed by fat student loans that you can't make ends meet, consolidating can give your cash flow a break.

Consolidation loans—and federal student loans—

Income–Contingent Repayment: Payments are based on your income and the total amount borrowed. Monthly payments are adjusted as your income changes, and the loan term is up to twenty-five years. At the end of the twenty-five years, any remaining balance will be forgiven. Keep in mind that that amount may be taxable.

Income–Sensitive Repayment: The loan term is ten years, and the monthly payment is a percentage of total monthly income before taxes.

Income–Based Repayment: This is new as of July 2009. It is like income–contingent repayment, but it limits the monthly payments to a lower percentage of discretionary income.

offer a variety of payment plans, so you can repay your balance over ten, twenty, even thirty years. The longer the loan term, the lower your monthly payments will be—but the more you'll pay overall in interest.

(On the flip side, you can also prepay on federal loans, just as you can prepay on your mortgage, which will bring the term of your loan down and lessen the blow of interest. Just be sure to include a note to your lender that the payment should be applied to the loan principle, and be aware that you will need to continue to make monthly payments just as you always have.)

How much do you stand to save each month? Lenders say that consolidators lower monthly payments by $150 on average. You can run your loans through the calculator at loanconsolidation.ed.gov (the Web site of Federal Student Aid) to get an exact number.

Found Money: $_____/month

Find the Money: Refinance Your Mortgage

We are in the midst of yet another refi boom, and if you want to take advantage of it you'd better act quickly. If you miss it, pay attention—opportunities to refinance tend to come around every few years. Just because the door to refinancing is closed to you today doesn't mean that it is closed to you forever.

There are a lot of different scenarios for which refinancing makes sense. You should consider it to cut your monthly payment when:

- Interest rates have fallen since you took out your loan, even by just one half to three quarters of a point.
- You missed the opportunity to refinance before. Don't kick yourself for missing the bottom of the market. If today's interest rates still make it possible for you to save enough money if you do the deal, then by all means do it.
- Your credit score has improved by twenty-five points or more. The lower your score was when you got your original mortgage, the more these improvements mean. For example, jumping from an already good score of 690 to an even better one of 715 would save you almost half a point. But jumping the same twenty-five points from a rotten score of 610 to a fair-to-middling 635 saves you a generous 1.1 percent.
- You've paid down enough of your mortgage to turn

a jumbo loan into a conforming loan. The interest rate on jumbo loans runs about one half of a percentage point higher than the rate on conforming loans. A loan for a single-family house is considered "jumbo" when you're borrowing more than $417,000 to $729,950. (The cap depends on where you live. In less expensive areas, the number is lower than in more expensive areas.)

So, how do you proceed? Call your current lender and ask about a "loan modification." That's an abbreviated form of a refi with less paperwork, fewer administrative hassles, and substantially lower costs. If you can't get your lender to play ball, then shop around.

There is no one source for the best rates on a mortgage these days. Check local lenders, online lenders, and mortgage brokers to see who can give you the best rate—and whether any of them can give you a rate that makes the deal worth doing. If you find a rate that works for you, *lock it in*. Rates can change as much as half a point from week to week. If they go up, you might find your window has closed.

Found Money: $_____/month

When a Refi Is Denied:
The Making Home Affordable Plan

What if you're told you can't refinance—even though you've paid your bills on time—perhaps because your house isn't worth what it was when you bought it? You may qualify for a loan modification under the 2009 Making Home Affordable plan, which will be in effect until June 10, 2010. It can bring your mortgage payment down to 31 percent of your gross monthly income by lowering your interest rate or extending your term. Are you eligible? You may be if you meet this criteria:

- You are the owner occupant of a one- to four-unit home
- The loan on your property is owned or securitized by Fannie Mae or Freddie Mac (to find out call 800-7-FANNIE or 800-FREDDIE, or go to fanniemae.com/loanlookup or freddiemac.com/mymortgage)
- At the time you apply, you are current on your mortgage payments (that means you haven't been more than thirty days late on your mortgage payment in the last twelve months or, if you have had the loan for less than twelve months, you have never missed a payment)
- The amount you owe on your mortgage is no more than 125% of the current value of your house
- You owe $729,750 or less on a one-unit property

continued

- You have income sufficient to support the new mortgage payments, and the refi improves the long-term affordability or stability of your loan. (How will you know? Your lender will give you a Good Faith Estimate that includes your new interest rate, new mortgage payment, and the amount you will pay over the life of the loan. Compare this with your current loan terms. If it is not an improvement, refinancing may not be right for you.) Refinancing from an adjustable- to a fixed-rate loan or eliminating higher-risk loan terms such as interest-only payments or balloon payments may also provide long-term stability.
- Your loan was originated on or before January 1, 2009
- Your mortgage payment (including taxes, insurance, and homeowners-association dues) is more than 31 percent of your gross (pretax) monthly income
- Your mortgage payment is not affordable, perhaps because of a significant change in income or expenses

For more information and to find out if your loan servicer is participating, go to makinghomeaffordable.gov. If you are having trouble communicating with your servicer, speaking with an HUD-approved housing counselor can help. Their assistance is free and you can reach them at 888-995-HOPE (4673).

Find the Money: Get Rid of Mortgage Insurance

Mortgage insurance (sometimes called PMI, for Private Mortgage Insurance) can be quite expensive. It's also not optional. You have to carry mortgage insurance if you put down less than 20 percent (when you buy a house. It costs you from $16 to $50 a month on every $100,000 you borrow in the form of a mortgage. And the way it works for loans made after July 1998 is that your lender has to cancel your mortgage insurance once you've accrued equity in your home of 78 percent.

The kicker comes when the value of your home appreciates rapidly, as it's done in many parts of the country over the last few years. All of that appreciation belongs to you, not the lender, and it may boost your ownership stake above the 20-percent mark. When that happens, you should try to get rid of your mortgage insurance.

As long as you have two full years of payments behind you, your first move should be to ask your lender to consider allowing you to drop the PMI. The lender will require you to have your house appraised, and you will have to pay for that appraisal, so you'll need to make a decision about whether it's worth spending some money up front to save some over the next couple of years. An appraisal will generally run in the $350 range. If you plan on staying in the house (and not refinancing) for more months than it would take you to pay that back, it makes sense to proceed. But you will want to have a good indication that you're right about the value of your home *before* you pay that appraisal money. So check the sale prices of comparable homes in your neighborhood: Visit a Web site such as domania.com or zillow.com, or call in a Realtor to find out what your house would list for.

The unfortunate thing is that your lender doesn't have to accept your appraisal. Your lender may decline it or may require a second opinion, and if you opt to get one, you have to pay for that, too.

Which brings me to option number two: Refinance. If you have been paying on your loan for less than two years, if you don't like your lender (for whatever reason), or if you get an indication from your lender that no matter how your appraisal comes in, getting rid of your mortgage insurance will be an uphill battle, refinancing is the other way to unload this costly burden. When you refinance, your house is appraised. That seals the value. As long as you borrow less than 20 percent of the value of your home in the form of a new mortgage (which you will automatically do as long as you don't pull cash out), there will be no insurance premium on the new loan.

How much could you save? You'll generally pay anywhere from a quarter of a percentage point to three quarters of a point of the money you borrow for mortgage insurance. The less you put down, the more of a risk the lender is taking and the higher that fraction will be. Mortgage insurance on adjustable-rate mortgages (ARMs) costs more than insurance on fixed-rate loans because ARMs are a riskier product for lenders (the default rate rises as the interest rate climbs). The easiest way to get an accurate assessment of how much this transaction will pad your pocket? See what you're paying now.

Found Money: $_____/month

How'd You Do?

So, how much found money were you able to come up with? Add up the numbers from the previous pages and let's get a sense of how you're doing.

At $100 a month, you're one third of the way there.
At $200 a month, you're over the halfway hump.

At $300 and change, you did it. In this one move, you did it.

Found Money: $_____/month

In any case, I'll bet you're feeling pretty good. Move on to the next chapter and I'll help you find even more money and feel even better.

Another Option for Seniors

Find the Money: Reverse Mortgages

Reverse mortgages are loans that allow you to borrow back the equity in your principal residence. Just as you once paid the bank, the bank instead pays you—and at the same time allows you to stay in your home. If you already have an existing mortgage on the home, you'll have to use some of the money you get from the reverse mortgage to pay that off.

If you think that sounds pretty appealing, you're not the only one. Homeowners have started taking out record numbers of these loans. Why? In part it's due to marketing. Campaigns to make seniors more aware of the availability of these loans have sparked interest. But seniors strapped by falling retirement-account balances and increases in the cost of medical care are also looking for new sources of cash to maintain their standards of living. Low mortgage rates haven't hurt either. They make it possible to draw more dollars out of your house than you've been able to get in prior years.

If you take out a reverse mortgage, you can get your payout in several ways: as a line of credit, a monthly payment, a lump sum, or some combination of all three. The line of credit is the most popular, but each has its benefits. A monthly payment is a guarantee of income for as long as you live in the house. A lump sum can be used to purchase an annuity that could provide you with lifetime income. If you choose the line of credit, you don't have to pay interest on money that you haven't withdrawn; in fact, your line of credit will *earn* interest while it's waiting to be used. (To get a sense of the sort of money you could reasonably expect to get from a reverse mortgage, check the calculator on the Web site of the National Reverse Mortgage Lenders Association at reversemortgage.org.)

That doesn't mean you won't have any expenses to pay. If you have a mortgage remaining on the house, part of your payout will go to pay off *that* loan before you can draw the first dime. And you'll still be responsible for taxes, homeowners insurance, and the general upkeep of the home. In fact, since the bank will actually own your house, you may be forced to pay the money back if you slide on these things. When you die or vacate the house, the amount you (or your heirs) will have to repay is the value of what you borrowed plus interest, but it

continued

can never exceed the total value (i.e., the sale price) of the home. If there's anything left after the sale of the home and the payment to the lender, you or your heirs get to keep it.

How much does it cost to get a reverse mortgage? In fees alone, you'll pay up to 10 percent of the amount you borrow. That's substantial, and it shouldn't be glossed over. Reverse mortgages are an expensive form of financing. According to John Rother, of the AARP, it is very difficult to get a reverse mortgage for less than $10,000 in fees—though the fees are often masked and rolled into the loan itself, which means you pay them by getting a little less from the lender each month. There are appraisal fees, origination fees, legal fees, the cost of a credit check, document-prep fees, etc. (*Note:* Some state and local governments offer lower-cost reverse-mortgage options, so check with your city's or county's housing department about options in your area.)

The good news is that although the costs are similar to those for a regular mortgage, the shopping process is much simpler. For 95 percent of people interested in a reverse mortgage, the best deal going is a federally insured Home Equity Conversion Mortgage (HECM), from the Federal Housing Authority, or FHA. (For a list of lenders that offer HECM loans, go to the Web site of the U.S. Department of Housing and Urban Development, hud.gov.) Unlike with traditional mortgages, interest rates on HECM loans are preset; they don't vary from lender to lender.

The remaining question: Is a reverse mortgage right for you? Before you can apply for one, you have to go through counseling with HUD. These counselors will explain how the loans work. They'll use software to run what-if scenarios so you can see how much money you'll receive. They'll explain what other options there may be. After you go through counseling, you can make a formal application. In general, however, reverse mortgages are best for:

- People who have considered moving and decided it's not right for them. It's important before you opt for a reverse mortgage to consider alternatives. For example, if you sold your house today, could you afford to buy another, smaller one and bank some money to live on? By taking the time to shop for condos and other places to live in your area, you may actually find something you like better.

- People who have discussed this with their families. Are you keeping your house because you really want it—or because you think your children do? If it's the latter, have you taken the time to confirm that with your kids? You might be surprised to learn they feel otherwise.

- People who've exhausted their other options for support. Borrowing money (and that's what you're doing with a reverse mortgage) shouldn't be considered until you deter-

continued

mine that there's no other source, such as Supplemental Security Income or additional Medicare or Medicaid benefits, for funds. Call the Department of Social Services in your area and speak to a counselor.

- People who have an immediate need for the money. If you don't need the income from a reverse mortgage today—even if you believe this is the solution for you—bide your time. As you age, the amount of money you'll qualify to draw will increase, making it an even more attractive option.

- People who plan to stay in their homes for at least five years. Even if you end up living in your home well past your life expectancy, the bank is obligated to keep paying you (if you chose a monthly sum) or to allow you to live there essentially rent-free. Also, if the value of your home hits a roadblock, the bank may end up paying you more than it's actually worth. But if you die, sell, or move within a few years of taking out a reverse mortgage, then it could be costly to you or your heirs—just as a traditional home loan would be, with its origination and closing costs and the cost of flipping the property in short order.

Just watch out for:

- Fees. As I said, the extra charges on this product can be very high. The fees are typically rolled into the mortgage, so you may not fully know what you're being charged. Ask to see a complete explanation of fees up front.

- Aggressive sales pitches. Reverse mortgages are sold for commission, much like life-insurance policies. Salespeople can come on so strong that the government requires you to meet with an approved counseling agency before signing on the dotted line. You can find a counselor at hud.gov.

- The notion that you should take out a reverse mortgage to pay for long-term-care insurance. You don't want to borrow to pay for an insurance policy.

Found Money: $_____/month

STEP 6

Find the Money:
Consolidating Your Debts

⌇

Consolidating your debts isn't the same thing as refinancing them. Consolidating, in technical terms, means taking debt from more than one source and rolling it up into a single loan with one—hopefully lower—interest rate. In practical terms, however, consolidating is often just an excuse to charge those paid-off credit cards right back up again, and that can be very, very dangerous. Many people consolidate by taking out a home equity loan or line of credit. They use the proceeds from that transaction to pay off their credit card debt. Others refinance their mortgages and simultaneously pull out some cash, using *that* money to pay down their credit card bills. Either way, you've taken an unsecured debt (one with no assets behind it) and turned it into a secured debt: You've put your home on the line to pay off your credit card bills.

What you got for taking this risk was the ability to pay off what was probably very high-rate credit card debt at a rate that's not only much, much lower but also tax deductible. Let's say you're carrying $20,000 of credit card debt at 18 percent. If you put aside $10 a day, it'll take you twenty-four years to pay that off. At 4 percent, you'll be able to do it in one third the time, *and* you get to deduct the interest you pay on your tax return. In other words, there are considerable advantages to consolidating. That's why it became such a popular option over the last decade.

Unfortunately, that's also why the option was abused. One third of people who use cash-out refis and home equity loans to pay off their credit card bills then proceed to charge their credit cards back up. Then they're not just right back where they started; they're in far worse shape, because now they have to pay back *both* loans.

So, you have to be sure of your willpower before you proceed with a consolidation loan. Do you have the ability to pay off those credit cards and then not use them again? Do you have the fortitude? Will you be able to tough it out, even if it means not buying the things you want—or, worse, the things your kids are asking you for? If you're not sure, then don't do this deal. *Don't.* Lower your interest rates as far as you can with the methods I described in the previous chapter. Work on your credit score so you can bring the rates down even further, but don't put yourself in the path of temptation. It's just not worth it.

If you decide to proceed, you need to do everything possible to keep yourself from falling off the wagon. Even if you're completely confident in your ability to steer clear of your plastic, you need to set up a system of roadblocks that will get in your way before you over-spend and overcharge. I'm dead serious about this. I don't care if you believe you've got the willpower of a Miss America contestant cutting carbs. Remember: One third of people who pay off their credit card bills with consolidation have big credit card bills again in no time. You don't think they all *planned* to climb back in the hole, do you?

So, what sort of safeguards are in order?

• Get rid of all but one or two low-rate credit cards. As I noted earlier, getting rid of *all* your cards will not be good for your credit score, part of which is based on the ratio of the credit you're using to your available credit. Closing accounts will cause that ratio to drop. But unless you're planning to apply for a mortgage or car loan in the next year, it's not a big deal. You're better off not having a walletful of temptation.

• Turn down credit–line increases on those cards—in fact, think about reducing the ones you have. You can get into only as much trouble as your credit lines will allow. Turning down a credit–line increase (or asking for a reduction) is as easy as calling the toll–free number on the back of your card.

• Take those credit cards out of your wallet and carry a debit card instead. If you're using a debit card, you can't spend money you don't have. (Go one step further and tell the bank you don't want overdraft protection. You may risk occasional embarrassment at checkout if you swipe your debit card and are denied because the funds aren't there, but you also won't incur a $39 over–limit fee.) Even frequent–flier–mile junkies have debit cards to choose from these days. No, you don't get quite as many miles, but it doesn't matter. They're not worth as much as they used to be anyway.

• Write checks and pay cash. For many people, it's tougher psychologically to part with their cash or write a check than it is to slide a piece of plastic through a little electronic slot. (That's why we spend more on credit than on debit, more on debit than with cash, and more in small bills than in big bills. The key to saving money? Carry only fifties!) It feels more real, and it is. Why? Because once the money's gone, it's really gone.

- Create small stashes for big goals. Let's say you decide you really want to go on vacation with your family at the end of the year. You're on track putting aside your $10 a day, and you don't want to let a short-term splurge get in the way of your long-term success. And you certainly don't want to charge it. How do you handle it? Create another savings pool. If you know that vacation is going to run $1,500 and you're five months out, then another $10 a day will get you to your goal. By rustling up the money beforehand, you'll be able to enjoy yourself and not feel guilty afterward.

- Tell your friends, family, and anyone else you're likely to (window) shop with what you're up to. If you clue your inner circle in to the fact that you're trying not to charge (indeed, that you're trying not to spend), they'll help you with that quest rather than suggest you spend your lunch hour trying on boots at Bloomingdale's. If online shopping is your particular weakness, unsubscribe to those mailing lists that tempt you—then tell your roommate, officemate, spouse, or anyone else who's likely to see you succumb. In fact, you may want to dub one of them your debt buddy—preferably someone who's facing the same financial challenges you are. Then you can talk your way through it.

Which Loan Do You Want?

Once your safeguards are in place and you're ready to proceed, you need to understand the consolidation landscape in order to get the best deal. That means understanding home equity loans and home equity lines of credit as well as cash-out refinances of your mortgage, starting with the fact that they are three very different animals. Here's a look at what they are, what they're good for, and where you'll typically find the best deals.

Home equity loans are fixed-rate loans. They're available in terms ranging from five years to fifteen years, though ten-year terms are the most common. When you take a home equity loan, you borrow the money all at once and start repaying it immediately.

- *They're best for* projects in which you need the money in one big chunk—such as redoing your kitchen.
- *Good deals* generally come from your bank (your local bank, in fact) or credit union. Closing costs vary widely, from about $300 to about $500, so shop around.

Home equity lines of credit (HELOCs) are variable–rate loans with interest rates that are usually tied to the prime rate (with a lifetime interest–rate cap of around 18 percent). They, too, typically have terms of ten years. Unlike home equity loans, however, having a *line* of credit means you don't have to borrow all the money at once. You receive the equivalent of a checkbook and withdraw (and of course pay back) funds as you need them.

- *They're best for* money you need to use over time. You pay interest only on the money you've withdrawn, which makes it a good use for costs you'll incur over several years, such as a home renovation you're approaching room by room, or college tuition. After all, why would you want to pay interest on the whole chunk of money when you're not using it all?
- *Good deals* are found by shopping around. Compare annual fees (generally around $50), and beware of

teaser rates. They're compelling, but you need to ask, Then what happens? Six months of very low interest means very little on a loan you're paying back over a decade.

A cash-out refinance involves going back to the mortgage well and drawing out additional equity, either that you've paid into the home or that has become yours through appreciation. For example, let's say you originally took out a $150,000 mortgage to buy a $200,000 home. Interest rates are lower than they were previously and you'd like to take advantage of that. But you also need $20,000 to pay back some high-rate credit card debt. You can refinance the loan for $170,000, which will give you the $150,000 you owe and the additional $20,000 at a lower interest rate. You're not taking out a second mortgage, as you are with HELOCs and home equity loans; you're replacing your first mortgage. This has advantages and disadvantages. One advantage is that as long as you aren't drawing out all the equity in your home—an option available during the early part of the millennium but thankfully not anymore—the interest rate will generally be lower than on the other options; another is that a greater amount of mortgage interest is tax deductible. A disadvantage is that you'll face additional costs—a new appraisal and closing costs—just like with any other refi.

- *They're best for* borrowers who've seen a drop in interest rates since they last took out a mortgage (or refinanced). It doesn't make sense to pay a higher interest rate on all the money you owe on your house. If rates have gone up and you still need to draw funds from your house, you're better off with a home equity loan or a HELOC, which will allow you to pay the higher interest rate on just the incremental chunk. One thing to watch out for: mortgage insurance. If you've moved beyond owing PMI (either by paying down more than 20 percent of your home or because of appreciation), another round of borrowing could put you right back in PMI territory. That amount alone may be more than the difference in interest rates between a HELOC/home equity loan and a refi. In that case, you're better off with the latter. And, particularly if you've been in your home more than five years, be wary of extending the term of your loan. See if you can use the lower rates to shorten your term to fifteen, twenty, even twenty-five years. You don't want to be paying off your mortgage as you head into your retirement years.

- *Good deals* are found by shopping around as you did when you originally got your mortgage. Check on-line sources, mortgage brokers, and your local bank or credit union before locking in your deal.

Tales of Life and Debt: A Step in the Right Direction— Consolidating Your Debts

Laurie, a member of my Web site, jeanchatzky.com, sent me this e-mail:

> I started with substantial savings of $16,000. Now I'm down to $800 with a great deal of credit card debt. I make a good salary, but I just can't seem to figure out how to start paying off my credit cards. One is at about $30,000 and I have others that are much smaller. I am basically paralyzed. . . . Can you please help me? I am extremely intelligent and embarrassed that I have so little financial sense.

A few days later, I gave Laurie a call. I learned that she is a paralegal, living on Sheppard Air Force Base in Texas. The $16,000 she was talking about came from her employer, who gave her a large bonus when he won an important case. She bought some furniture with about a quarter of the money, then put the rest in savings with the intent of paying down her debt.

But she got sidetracked. Actually, she got sick. Her doctor found a tumor that he suspected was uterine cancer. In the end, thankfully, it was benign, but the combination of increased medical expenses and time spent not working did a number on her savings. After she had surgery, she was left with a huge credit card bill and only $2,000 in the bank. Not surprisingly, her financial situation put a damper on the happiness she was feeling over her health.

In looking over the numbers together, though, we found that her situation wasn't as bad as she feared. First of all, Laurie and her husband, who's in the military, don't have a mortgage. That means all of their earnings can go to paying their bills and other living expenses. She spends more than she has to on eating out and clothing—areas in which she's willing to cut back. They are currently paying $9,000 a year in college tuition for their son. But since he's halfway through his junior year, there is also an end in sight. The $6,000 a year they're paying for car insurance—not for their car, for their insurance!—is exorbitant, but Laurie admits she hasn't shopped around for a better deal. And the interest rates on their credit cards are higher than they have to be. Again, Laurie hadn't even attempted to bring them down.

That was the assignment I gave her: Reduce your costs in all of these areas. She took it on with gusto. In fact, it wasn't even twenty-four hours later that she sent me the following e-mail:

> *My husband and I both realize that my debts are the ones we need to work on since his are small in comparison, and we can surely work on his after we've learned how to manage mine. We both want desperately to get our debt under control so we can purchase a house when he retires from the military in 4–5 years.*

As I told Laurie, she can take comfort in knowing that she's taken a step in the right direction.

STEP 7

Find the Money: Spending Less

W hy do we spend money? Sometimes it's because we need something. We need to fix the
leak in the roof. We need a car (or other form of transportation) to get us to and from work. We need day
care for our children so we can go to those jobs. We
need to put food on the table and appropriate clothing on our bodies. We need a telephone to keep in
touch with our offices and our spouses, to call the
authorities in an emergency. We need decent medical
care.

But mostly we spend because we *want* things. We
want to go out to dinner because we've just had a long
day or week. We want a cell phone in addition to our

landline because we want to be reachable anytime, any-where. We want to look better and feel better than we feel right now—and we think that spending money on new shoes, a new set of golf clubs, new makeup, or a new bag will help us do just that. When you stop and think about it, you have to admit that's where a great deal of your money goes.

We need certain things—and we want others. That's the top explanation for where every bit of your money goes. But if you're one of those people who feels they shop a little too much (and come on, who doesn't feel like that occasionally?), there's probably a more deep-rooted reason for your behavior.

Sue Eccles and Helen Woodruffe-Burton, two British researchers, took an academic look at why we go shopping. They believe that when we shop for anything other than the true essentials, it's because we're missing something else in our lives. The catchphrase for this behavior is "retail therapy," but in academic circles it's called "compensatory consumption." And they've put their fingers on seven reasons why we engage in it:

• We're bored—with our lives, our looks, our cars and appliances. When we shop out of boredom, we're looking for a pick-me-up.

- We're depressed and need an escape from reality. Shopping is a more socially acceptable escape from dealing with deep unhappiness than alcohol or drugs. New research has shown, however, that shopping can be just as unhealthy.

- We want to "get a life." We're underwhelmed with the look and shape our life has taken, so we spend to produce a better-looking, fuller-feeling one.

- We want to improve our mood. Shopping, for some people, brings a feeling of excitement, the "high" of getting a good deal. Shopping is a mission. The idea of a trip to the mall or your favorite boutique sets your toes tingling, a little like a caffeine buzz.

- We are trying to assert our independence over our parents and then, later, our partners. In marriages and other relationships that aren't functioning well, one spouse may overspend to teach the other that "you don't own me."

- We want to feel more attractive. We are convinced that if only we had that dress (that tie, those shoes), we'd look one hundred times better.

- We're on autopilot. It's been so long since we *didn't* drop that $5 a day on coffee and a bagel that we do it without thinking about it—even when we're not hungry; even when we don't really want it. We get into patterns with our shopping just as we do with many other things in our lives. Sometimes, those patterns are tough to break.

I share these reasons with you because I believe that knowing why you're engaging in a particular behavior can help you to get a grip on it. Until you understand why you've got ten pairs of similar black pants in your closet that you really don't need, for example, or stacks of DVDs that you have yet to watch, it's tougher to stop yourself from purchasing the next unnecessary item.

Women, research shows, are more likely to spend on nonessentials (and therefore overspend) than men. That's probably because we're the ones who do most of the spending overall. Since the nineteenth century, women have done about 80 percent of our country's shopping. That ratio remains fairly consistent, even today. Originally, we gravitated to shops because they—unlike pubs and bars—were one of the few places a woman could go alone without worrying about her safety or her reputation. Department stores caught on to these shopping patterns and, as they developed, out-fitted themselves to attract women who had money to spend. Today, though, it's not just in the stores that women are outspending men; it's online. Unfortunately, women are also less likely to haggle. According to research for the book *Women Don't Ask: Negotiation and the Gender Divide*, by Linda Babcock and Sara Laschever (Princeton University Press), female car buyers will pay as much as $1,353 (yikes!) more to *avoid* negotiating the price of a car.

What we're going to do in this step is go through the lists of all the different things you spend money on each month. For each item, you need to ask yourself, Is this necessary? If it's not, then I want you to rank it high priority, medium priority, or low priority. (I'm going to share with you how I'd rank the items as well, and although it's perfectly fine for your rankings to be different from mine—you and I probably do have different needs—it's not okay for everything you spend money on to be a high priority. Your expenditures should split fairly equally among the three categories. Be sure you fill in your calculated savings on the blank after "Found Money" for each item.) Then, we'll see if there's a way to trim your costs and by how much. At the end of the exercise, you'll see how much money you were able to free up.

(*Note:* Don't just skip over the line for "Other." I have put into this work sheet just about everything I could think of, but as I said, you and I have different lives. This exercise works only if you're really honest about where your money is going today.)

Fixed Expenses

• *Rent/Mortgage*: High priority. Consider refinancing. See Step 5.

Found Money: $_____/month

• *Common charges (condo fees, etc.)*: High priority. Non-negotiable. No found money here.

• *Car payment 1*: High priority. Consider refinancing. See Step 5.

Found Money: $_____/month

• *Car payment 2*: Medium priority. A second car, no doubt, really makes your life easier, but do you need it? Could one of you drive the other to work or drop the other off at a bus or train station? Could you car-pool with a coworker? I know this means trading convenience for savings, but that's what this entire exercise is about. If you need the car, consider refinancing as a way to save money on your loan. If you're driving a relatively new or expensive car, consider selling it, paying off your loan, and buying a cheaper, older model. That will save you money each month. For how–to information, see Step 5.

Found Money: $_____/month

• *Car payment 3:* Low priority. A third car? I've heard a number of explanations for why this is necessary. You need a car for the sitter to drive or for your high schooler to get back and forth to his or her activities. I'm dubious. But if your high schooler truly needs this car, then he or she should be helping to pay for it by earning money to foot the bill for insurance, gas, even a portion of the payment if possible. Still, maybe there's another way. Maybe your spouse could drop you off at work and your teen could pick you up. Again, if you really do need it, refinance the loan if you haven't al–ready. But you're going to need to trim elsewhere.

Found Money: $_____/month

• *Train ticket, parking, and other commuting expenses:* High priority. Have you run the numbers to see which is the most economical way to commute? By bus? By train? By car? Have you shopped around for the cheapest parking solution? Have you looked into carpooling so you don't have to pay for parking every day? Call your benefits department to see if your company has a transportation savings account, which works like a flexible-spending account. It allows you to pay for transportation expenses, including parking, with pre-tax dollars, which will save you one quarter to one third of the cost.

Found Money: $_____/month

• *Child support:* High priority. Your child deserves your support. However, if you are in a situation in which you cannot pay, notify your child-support agency immediately. If you've become ill or disabled and can't work, you can ask the court to review your support order to restructure or reduce your payments. No found money here.

• *Alimony:* High priority. If you've agreed to pay alimony, then of course you should pay it. However, you should also know that the courts believe failing to pay child support is generally much worse than failing to pay alimony. No found money here either.

• *Back taxes:* High priority. Call the IRS and see if you can work out a payment schedule that makes sense for you. They are notoriously flexible if they know that they'll eventually get their money. The important thing to stress is that you want to pay but you're having trouble making ends meet right now.

• *Student-loan payment:* High priority. Would consolidating offer you any relief? See Step 6.

Found Money: $_____/month

• *Credit card payments:* High priority. As we've established, only *after* you dig out of credit card debt will you be able to make true progress with the rest of your financial goals. That makes this a high-priority line item. Work to lower your interest rates to make payoff faster and less expensive. See Step 5.

Found Money: $_____/month

• *Utilities:* High priority. But there's much you can do to save. Lower your thermostat; even a single degree will help. Do the same with your water heater. And in the summer, turn the thermostat on the A/C up a bit. Call your utility provider and ask about an energy audit to reduce your costs. Some do this. If yours does, you can find an independent auditor at natres net.org. An auditor will go through your home and pinpoint areas where you're bleeding energy—and money. Use compact-fluorescent bulbs instead of regular lightbulbs (replacing ten will save $44 a year). When your appliances die, buy better ones (buying new ones before you need them is a spending exercise, not a saving one) and then take care of them. A home outfitted with appliances that have the Energy Star logo will cost 30 percent less a year to run than one without. To help your heater or furnace work more efficiently, check the air filters once a month and clean (washable ones are available) or replace them if they're dirty (that can save $50 in heating a year). Buying a thermostat that adjusts automatically at night can knock another 10 percent off your utility bills. Caulk and seal or put weather stripping around drafty windows and doors. And unplug appliances when you're not using them. (Using power strips enables you to plug many things into a single outlet and then unplug just one.)

Found Money: $_____/month

• *Health club:* Low priority. This is one of those things you pay for every month that you may not even use. If you don't go more than once a week, you absolutely need to cancel your membership. Even if you do go, consider canceling your membership or at least putting it on hold until you dig out. Could you pay a less-expensive rate to take a class occasionally? Could you run or walk (or engage in some other free pursuit) outside? If you feel you really need a gym (and I understand that for some people it's a matter of sanity), check with your company's benefits department. Many offer health–club discounts. Also look to see if your health insurer offers any sort of reimbursement. Then shop around to see if you can find a better deal. Once you've secured one (it won't be difficult), go back to the gym you belong to and see if you can use your new rate to bargain for a discount. Explain that you may have to leave unless they can give you a break on the monthly dues. If that doesn't work, you'll have to switch.

Found Money: $_____/month

• *Internet, phone, and cable:* Medium priority. Just as you're likely in the habit of shopping around for phone service, you can do the same with Internet, phone, and cable. Call your provider and use the announcement of new competition in your neighborhood to help you shop for a better deal. Bundling these services together should help you get a better rate—so should trimming channels you can do without.

Found Money: $_____/month

• *Cell phone/wireless:* High priority if you give up your landline; medium if you don't. About one quarter to one third of Americans have cut the cord and are relying on their cell phones for communication. That's a good place to start. The next is to pick up the phone, call your wireless provider, and ask whether your plan is right for your needs. Although it's tough to get out of your contract without paying a fee, it's easy to scale back on the services you're buying. Stop texting, or buy an unlimited package—whichever saves you the most money. Try to put all the users in your house on a single plan. Take advantage of new offers to add numbers to your "circle" or "friends and family" so it won't cost you more to talk to them. Then do it again six months later. The calculators at myrateplan.com or lowermybills.com can help you figure out where your best deals might be.

Found Money: $_____/month

• *Child care/babysitter:* High priority. Set up a dependent-care spending account through your employer (the vast majority of companies offer this option), which allows you to pay for day care using pretax dollars. That move alone can save you 30 percent on your tab. And if one of you is out of work, it makes no sense to employ a babysitter for children of school age. You can look for work that needs you from eight a.m. until the kids get out at three o'clock. Then you can work for the family.

Found Money: $_____/month

• *Health insurance*: High priority. Call your benefits department and see if there is a less expensive plan you could switch to within your company. If you and your spouse are both working for employers that offer coverage, it probably will make sense for each of you to take coverage from your own company (unless one employer covers families for free) rather than doubling up. If you are paying for your own insurance, go to ehealthinsurance.com, a Web site that sells health insurance directly to consumers, to see if it's possible to switch to a less expensive plan. A high-deductible plan will save you the most money while preventing a health scare from bankrupting you.

Found Money: $_____/month

• *Homeowners (or renters) and auto insurance*: High priority. If it's been a while since you shopped around for these coverages, you're probably paying more than you have to. Call an independent insurance agent (one who can quote you policies from a variety of carriers) and shop on the Internet as well. Buying both of these policies from a single carrier can net you a significant discount. There are also discounts if you've stopped smoking, improved security in your home, been with a particular insurer for more than three years, or hit your fifty-fifth birthday (seniors generally stay home more, spend more time maintaining their homes, and drive less; insurers reward them for this). But you'll get the biggest savings by raising your deductibles. Your deductible is the amount of money you'll have to pay out of pocket *before* your insurance coverage kicks in. Most deductibles start at $250. If you raise yours to $500, you'll save up to 12 percent. Go even higher—to $1,000—and you can save up to 24 percent. You can go higher still and save 30 percent or more, but be sure that you don't go too high for your wallet.

Found Money: $_____/month

• *Life insurance:* High priority. If you're single and have no dependents (either kids or older parents you support), you don't need life insurance. Unless it's coverage your company provides for free, get rid of it. If you have dependents, then life insurance becomes a high-priority item, but you have to buy smart, which means that if you're in cost-cutting mode, you shouldn't be buying any form of permanent insurance (whole life, universal

life, or annuities). You should be buying term life insurance. Term life insurance is a death benefit with nothing
else attached. It covers you only while you pay for it
(generally for a term of ten to thirty years), and for that
reason it's much, much cheaper than permanent insurance. The other way to find cheaper rates is to buy
group insurance, generally through your employer. You
may have to pay for it, but it can be less expensive than
comparable plans you'll find shopping alone. What if
you've already started paying for a cash–value/perma-
nent policy and you're having trouble making the payments? Call your insurer. You may have the option to
convert the policy to a term life policy based on the
cash you've already accumulated. You can also cash out.
You'll no longer be covered by the insurance, but you
can use the money to pay down your existing debts,
and then replace the policy with cheaper term life.

(*Note:* Don't cancel your existing insurance policy
until you secure a new one. You will have to undergo
a physical exam for a new policy. If your health has
changed for the worse, you may find the cost of a new
policy prohibitive—or you could find that you don't
qualify at all.)

Found Money: $_____/month

• *Regular prescriptions:* High priority. Yes, these are non-negotiable items. Yes, you can also save money. How? By making sure you buy generic drugs rather than name brands where available. If you're on Medicare, obtaining one of the new drug–discount cards can save you 10 to 17 percent annually—more if you're a low-income individual. Consider ordering from an online pharmacy as well, where you can often cut your costs substantially.

Found Money: $_____ /month

• *Payments for other purchases such as furniture and appliances:* Medium priority. Although you of course want to make these payments, the fact is you can probably let them slide for a while without worrying about re-possession. In order to repossess your property, the lawyers at the National Consumer Law Center point out, the lender has to get permission to come into the house, and you're unlikely to give them that. It also costs merchants so much to go through the exercise of getting back your property that many will decide it's not worth it. If you're having trouble making these payments, call your local credit union (if you don't belong to one, go to cuna.org to find one that will have you as a member) and see if you can refinance the debt through them with an unsecured personal loan. You'll pay a much lower interest rate and get rid of the other garbage—such as credit insurance—that was probably packaged with the loan. Even if you face pre-payment penalties (and you might), you can probably save money. If prepayment penalties are so onerous that you don't want to switch lenders, call your current lender to ask for a reduction in the interest rate and cancel any insurance that goes with the loan.

Found Money: $_____/month

• *Housekeeper:* Low priority. Perhaps you could cut visits in half if not entirely.

Found Money: $_____/month

• *Lawn care:* Low priority. Again, this becomes a do-it-yourself item.

Found Money: $_____/month

• *Private school:* Medium priority. Most private schools (and private nursery schools) have someone on staff to deal with the issue of financial aid. (You're not the only one in this boat!) Make an appointment to meet with that person to see if you can obtain financial assistance. Particularly if your child has been thriving at the school, many administrators will do everything they can to help you get through these hard times. Check other resources for scholarships and aid as well, such as your employer, your clergy, or the Internet. If your child is in this school because of a special learning (or other) need, talk to your state education department about whether assistance is available. If all of these avenues fail, you will have to consider moving your child to public school.

Found Money: $_____/month

• *Tutoring:* Medium priority. Talk to your school principal. Explain that you're having financial difficulties but you'd like to maintain the tutoring for your child. He or she may have suggestions for free or low-cost tutoring in your area. If you're receiving tutoring through a large-scale program, talk to the director about a reduction in price until you get on your financial feet.

Found Money: $_____/month

• *After-school programs/sports for your kids:* Medium priority. First, let's differentiate between after-school programs whose purpose is to allow you to finish your workday and those that are simply extracurricular activities. The first are necessities (though you should look into whether financial assistance is available or if there's a lower-cost option, for which tax breaks may be available if your children are age thirteen or younger). The second are extras. I know; I have two children. I know that although you're willing to cut back for yourself, cutting back for your children can be heartbreaking. But this is an area in which you absolutely need to look at trying to save some money. Perhaps you could switch from a basketball program at a private facility to a cheaper one with your town's recreation department. Maybe you can drop two of four music lessons per month. Again, always ask if aid is available. If there are activities your kids constantly fight you about attending, now's the time to drop them. If the children in question are teenagers, now is a good time to talk to them about contributing to the cost of their activities by babysitting or getting a part-time job.

Found Money: $_____/month

• *Church, synagogue, or other religious-center expenses:* Low priority. Your house of worship is one area that will almost definitely cut you a break. Schedule an appointment with a clerical leader; explain your financial situation and that you'll start paying again as soon as you're able.

Found Money: $_____/month

• *Summer camp:* Medium priority. Again, if the only way you're able to work during the summer is by find-ing a camp program for your kids, camp becomes a necessity. Financial assistance and tax breaks are often available. Shop around for a good program at a good price and then apply for it. (*Note:* Any expense you incur for a child under age thirteen that allows you to go to work may be deducted as part of the dependent-care credit, which is worth approximately $2,000 to your bottom line each year).

Found Money: $_____/month

• *Other:* As you went through and tracked your monthly fixed expenses, you probably came up with several that are not listed here. Use the strategies we've discussed to try to trim your costs in those areas.

Found Money: $_____/month

Total Found Money from Fixed Expenses:

$_____/month

Now it's time to attack your variable expenses. Except for groceries and gasoline, these are not going to be high-priority items—certainly not as high as paying your rent or your mortgage. That means your first step should be to see if you can free up enough money to repay your debts by shopping around. There's more flexibility there than you may think. The Consumer Literacy Consortium recently engaged a group of students at Virginia Tech for an exercise in comparison shopping. They had the students make three phone calls each to see if they could get a better deal on car rentals, color TVs, and plane tickets. They did incredibly well. After three phone calls the savings on car rentals averaged 10 percent; on televisions, 20 percent; and on plane tickets, 50 percent. It also means you have to be willing to give up certain items—certainly not every item on the list, and certainly not forever.

But a big part of this exercise is focusing on what *things* in your life are most important to you. It involves setting priorities and making conscious choices. Those are the only ones you should be spending money on in this debt-repayment stage. If you're having trouble discriminating, ask yourself the question this way: Which *things* are more important than your future?

To get a sense of how much money you're finding in

each category, figure out how much you have been spending on average each month. Then figure out how much you think you could spend on a budget.

Variable Expenses

• *Groceries:* High priority. Of course you need to eat. But, in our time–starved world, it's very easy to fall into the trap of shopping meal by meal. That can be almost as expensive as eating in a restaurant. Likewise, making lunches for your kids to take to school (and for you to take to work) will always be less expensive than buying them. The solution is to do what your mother (or maybe your grandmother) told you to do: Plan out a week's worth of meals. Include a day or so of left–overs in your schedule. Then make a list and shop for just what you need. You'll spend less on convenience foods if you try to shop only the outside aisles of the supermarket. That'll net you produce, dairy, meat, and fish. If you venture inside, make sure you're going for a particular item or another. Then pay close attention to what gets eaten (and what gets wasted) in your house. Clipping coupons for items you use (not for items you want to try) can save money as well, particularly if you use them at stores that offer double or triple the value. (You'll find 80 percent of the valuable coupons in the Sunday circulars in your paper—but more online at Web sites like couponmom.com.) And be sure to join the loyalty program of every supermarket in town. That way, no matter which market you decide to patronize that week, you'll get the best prices. You may, with this new meal-planning strategy, actually spend a little more in this category the first couple of weeks as you're loading up on spices and other ingredients. Don't worry, you'll recoup the money because you won't be eating out as much.

Found Money: $_____/month

• *Restaurant meals:* Low priority. How many nights a month do you eat in a restaurant? Cut that number in half with the understanding that if that doesn't move you close enough to your goal, you may have to cut further. Also, be sure that when you do dine out, you don't do it in a way that sabotages your money-saving goals.

Found Money: $_____/month

• *Takeout:* Low priority. Takeout is a habit more than anything else. You're not getting the experience of sitting in a nice restaurant and being served; you're opening a brown paper bag and wolfing down a sandwich at your desk. Think carefully about which of these expenses can go. Can you stomach the coffee from the office pot? That's 75 cents a cup if you've been buying from the cart on the corner; $3 a cup if you've been drinking a designer brand. Can you handle bringing your lunch from home rather than buying it from the local sandwich shop? You could free up your $10 a day right there. And how much money are you actually dropping into those soda and candy machines in the company lounge? You know, they're not very good for your waistline, either.

Found Money: $_____/month

• *Gasoline:* High priority. If your car doesn't call for premium gasoline, use regular. Don't skimp on the oil changes that keep it running efficiently. By all means, carpool. You can find the cheapest per-gallon prices in your neighborhood at Web sites like gaspricewatch .com. (And the next time you're in the market for a car, consider getting one that doesn't guzzle.)

Found Money: $_____/month

• *Other medical expenses (appointments that aren't reimbursed):* High/medium priority. If you need to see a doctor, you need to see a doctor. This isn't the time, however, to be spending large sums of unreimbursed money on cosmetic procedures of any kind—for your eyes, your skin, or your teeth. For those expenditures you do need to make, signing up for a flexible-spending account at work allows you to pay for unreimbursed medical expenses with pretax dollars. The hitch is that you have to ballpark the amount you'll spend at the beginning of each year—and if you don't use that amount, you lose it. Call your benefits department to see if this is a possibility for you.

Found Money: $_____/month

• *Clothing, shoes, and accessories:* Medium/low priority. I'm not suggesting you never buy another pair of pants or shoes, but you need to think of these purchases in terms of whether they're actually needed—and how much you absolutely have to spend on them. New $20 sneakers for your child whose feet won't stop growing? Needed. New $50 name-brand sneakers for your child whose feet won't stop growing? I don't think so. A new black dress to wear to your cousin's wedding? Not if you have three others in the closet. It doesn't really matter that hemlines have moved. Shorten it. And know that if you're not the bride, no one will be looking at you anyway. If you're looking to trim expenses rather than cut them out entirely, you need to know how to shop the sales. Timing is everything when it comes to not paying full price. Generally, department stores take their first markdowns two months after merchandise has been on the shelves. In chain stores, those markdowns come even sooner. Generally, first markdowns run 20 to 30 percent. If the item you're after looks to be in short supply (or if you're a tough size), that's the time to buy. If there's ample stock, you can take comfort in knowing that two weeks down the road, items will be reduced (from the original price) by 40 percent. By the time third markdowns roll around (another two weeks later), you'll see prices of up to 70 percent off. Interestingly, personal shoppers say you'll do better shopping at department stores than boutiques. Not only do they have more lenient return policies; they're more inclined to discount because if items don't sell, designers will give them credits for future merchandise.

Found Money: $_____/month

• *Entertaining/entertainment:* Medium priority. If you take all the fun out of your life, this is not going to be a plan that you're going to be able to stick with for very long. That's why the goal here—as in many of the other categories—is to trim expenses, not eliminate them. So instead of restaurant meals, invite friends in and do a potluck. Or fill your friends in on the fact that you're trying to budget and they'll naturally start to suggest drinks instead of dinner, or the local Italian joint instead of the chic and pricey brasserie. Challenge yourself to come up with cheaper ways of enjoying yourself: Ice-skate outside rather than indoors; show movies on pay-per-view ($3.95 and everyone can watch!) instead of going out to the movies or theater, or signing up for a video-rental service that charges you every month even when you're not using it. Take day trips to the nearest beach rather than weekend overnighters. And if you spend more than you'd like for Saturday-night sitters, try piggybacking with friends: You take care of their kids one week; they take care of yours the next.

Found Money: $_____/month

• *Travel:* Low priority. Yes, you have to have some fun, but while you're trying to cut back, this is one big-ticket expense that can be sharply curtailed. If you generally vacation both summer and winter, think about cutting out one of those trips—at least while you're getting on your feet. Particularly during high (read: crowded) season, vacationing at home ("stayca-tioning") can be just as fun—and much more restful. The key to not blowing the budget is shopping smart when you do venture out. If you're buying airline tick-ets, you're better off buying very early—or very late. On the most competitive routes, advertised sale fares disappear quickly, so you want to jump on board as soon as you see them in the morning paper (or your e-mail). Last-minute deals are more prevalent if you're willing to travel places many vacationers won't go or you can be flexible on the days you're willing to leave and return (even if that means pulling your kids out of school a day early). When booking a hotel room, use the Internet to pinpoint where you want to stay and at what price, then call the hotel directly to ask if there's a better deal available. If you've racked up airline miles, using them for hotel stays is one way to maxi-mize their value.

Found Money: $_____/month

• *Gifts:* Medium priority. My mother always said it's the thought that counts. But she also taught me that you never show up at a party or someone's house empty-handed. The trick is to split the difference. If your kids are attending birthday party after birthday party, think about declining the invitations from the kids they really don't know or play with. Then buy great, inexpensive gifts in bulk whenever and wherever you find them. Warehouse stores can be great sources for these. I recently picked up a huge set of really cool markers that were selling for $5.95 (I got ten packages). Other tactics: Go in with friends or relatives to slice the cost of gifts in half. Plan a grab bag for the holidays so that you're buying only for a single person, not everybody. Decide to make a contribution to a friend's favorite charity. (Nobody needs to know how much or how little you gave.) Resist the urge to try to keep pace with what your more affluent (less indebted) friends are buying you. Someone has to break what often becomes a ridiculously lavish cycle; it might as well be you.

Found Money: $_____/month

• *Newspapers and magazines:* Low priority. First, cancel anything you're not reading. Second, see what you can read for free on the Internet. Third, if you buy (and read) it every day or every month, subscribe—forgo the newsstand, which is three times the price.

Found Money: $_____/month

• *Books:* Low priority. Use the library.

Found Money: $_____/month

• *CDs/music/DVDs:* Low priority. Again, use the library. Or swap what you have for what you want at Web sites like swaptree.com.

Found Money: $_____/month

• *Grooming expenses (manicures, blow-outs):* Low priority. Other than getting a haircut when you need it, this is one category that can be slashed to nearly nothing. The $10 you spend on a manicure every week adds up to $520 toward your debt (or savings) by the end of the year. So . . . learn how to do your own nails, straighten your own hair (I did), tweeze your own eyebrows, and wax your own legs.

Found Money: $_____/month

• *Pets:* Medium priority. Before you give in to your child's pet craving, understand the expense you're taking on. The care and feeding of a cat or small dog can run to $700 or $800 annually; for large dogs, double that. If you're trying to minimize expenses, not venturing into pet ownership at all (save, per-haps, a goldfish) is a smarter move. If you already have a pet, you can minimize their prescription–drug costs by buying medications through your own drugstore or online rather than through your vet. Local pet stores holding clinics for simple health–care needs such as shots will be cheaper than a vet appointment. Buy food in bulk at warehouse stores or online.

Found Money: $_____/month

• *Other*: The same rules apply. Pare back where you can; do without where you have to.

Found Money: $_____/month

Found Money from Variable Expenses:

$_____/month

Total Found Money (Fixed + Variable):

$_____/per month (30 days)

TOTAL FOUND MONEY/DAY: $_____

So, how did you do? Did you find your $10 a day? Did you find more? If so, that's terrific. You can move on to Step 9, page 163, which will tell you how to make sure that money gets where it needs to be. If you didn't free up enough cash, go to Step 8. There we'll talk about other ways to find the necessary money: making some hard choices, selling assets, and earning more.

STEP 8

Find the Money: Making Hard Choices, Selling Assets, Earning More

W hat if you get to this point in the book and you haven't freed up enough money to save that $10 a day? Then you have three choices. You can go back through some of the bigger-ticket items in the previous chapter—the ones you thought were nonnegotiable—and try to reduce them further. You can go through your home and your possessions and see if there's anything of value to sell by having a garage sale, listing items on Web sites such as eBay, or using a consignment shop or broker. You can try to earn more money, either in your current job or, more likely, by taking on a second one. The other alternatives? Credit counseling, debt settlement, and bankruptcy. You're not there yet. We'll get to those drastic measures toward the end of the book. For now, let's see what else you can accomplish on your own.

Making Hard Choices

Sometimes cutting back on what you're spending on takeout and turning off lights is all you need to do to begin paying down your debt. Sometimes that doesn't make a big-enough dent, so you need to look at the line items that are costing you the most money: housing, your car(s), education, and so on. Your own detailed listing of your expenses will open your eyes to the areas that are hurting your chances of paying back your debts and becoming wealthy. It's time to take a closer look. Among the things you may want to consider:

Moving. Is your housing sabotaging your ability to make ends meet? I know it's hard to hear, but for a lot of people, the answer is yes. During the last decade or so, we were so afraid that if we didn't buy *right now* we'd be priced out of the only neighborhood we wanted to live in. We were afraid that if we didn't bid *so much* for that charming three-bedroom Cape we'd lose it, just as we lost the last four houses we wanted. But it may be that selling your house is a solution you have to consider. I know the conventional wisdom is that your house is the asset you'll retire on (and often retire *in*), that it's the most valuable asset in your portfolio. But unless you can afford to make the payments, it's also the one that can be your Achilles' heel. It may be *necessary* to trade down, to swap a larger house for something more manageable and less expensive. You also may need to consider renting for a while. As long as you can keep the cost of moving reasonable (recruit your friends), renting will save you the cost of homeowners insurance. (You'll need renters insurance, but it's much cheaper.) You'll save on yard care, and depending on where you relocate to, you may be able to cut your commuting costs as well. And rent itself is cheaper: The average rent payment in this country is 24 percent lower than the average mortgage payment, according to *The Wall Street Journal*. In other words, if this is the decision you have to make, now is a pretty good time to make it. I'm not saying that you shouldn't own a house. Owning a house and paying it off is a big step toward wealth and financial security. A paid-off house is like a supplemental savings account—an asset you can sell to raise funds or draw upon if and when you need it. I'm saying that if you can't make ends meet, perhaps you shouldn't own *this* house at *this* time.

Getting rid of a car. If you dig down deep and consider it, there probably is another, less expensive way for you to get back and forth to work each day. Think about what you did when gas prices were over $4 a gallon, in the summer of 2008. Did you carpool with a neighbor or colleague? Did you arrange to work one day a week from home? Then do more. By going without a car for a while, you could save the cost of paying for the car itself, its upkeep, gasoline, auto insurance, and parking. And if you can't go without, how about trading in your pricey car for one that runs just fine but is used and less luxurious? I understand that making both of these choices seems like a huge hassle, but every hard choice you make requires some form of sacrifice. If you haven't been able to bring your budget in line so far, the question is not whether you're going to have to make hard choices; it's *which* hard choices you are going to make.

Putting your children in public school. The thought of moving your children from one school to another can be overwhelming. (For some of us, the thought of taking just about anything valuable from our kids elicits the same reaction.) But I just want to tell you from experience—it's not so bad. I moved four times when I was growing up, and as a result I went to elementary school in Wisconsin, middle school in Indiana, and high

appraised by a certified appraiser. The key to get–
ting an *accurate* appraisal is hiring an appraiser
who is not in the business of selling the item. If
the appraiser could possibly sell the item, he or
she has a financial incentive to undervalue it. That
would enable him or her to make more on the
transaction. If it's a household item that's not
worth having appraised, you can get an accurate
idea of fair market value by seeing what similar
items are selling for in classified advertisements or
on eBay.

- *Consider where you're likely to get the best price.* It may not
  be where you think. For example, the best prices on
  used cars rarely come to you via a dealer trade–in.
  These days dealers make so little money on new
  cars, they have to make it up on used cars (i.e., your
  trade–in), financing, and service. You may do better
  selling it yourself—but there will be the aggravation
  of advertising it, showing it, and having people
  come to your house to see it.

- *Decide whether you'll sell it yourself or use a broker.* Just as
  there are real estate brokers to sell homes, there are
  individuals who will sell just about anything for a
  cut. Professional estate sellers and liquidators (in the
  phone book under "liquidators") will come in, as–

sess what you have to sell, and tell you if they can get rid of it for you—though they typically won't take lots worth less than a few thousand dollars. If you're dealing with smaller potatoes and you don't want to go it alone, you can use individuals—often those with eBay's "PowerSeller" designation—who will auction off your merchandise on the Internet. You hand it over; they hand you a check for 50 to 70 percent of what they net. The big question is, do you have the time, skill, and inclination to do it yourself? If not, by all means hand it over, make the money, and put it to better use.

- *Whatever you're selling, take the time to make it look good.* If it's a car, clean it thoroughly, including the engine (consider having your car professionally detailed if you can come up with the cash), and have your local body shop take out any noticeable dents or scratches. If it's an item you're selling on eBay, make sure you post a good-looking photo (or perhaps several taken from different angles).

- *Be cautious about the transaction.* Don't take a personal check. Accept cash, cashier's checks, or money orders only. If a buyer tells you they need a day or two to obtain that cashier's check, make sure you get a deposit in cash.

How to Have a Great Garage Sale

There are entire books written on how to make the most money from a garage sale, but the body of advice seems to boil down to a few commonsense tips:

- *Start with a plan.* Pick a date at least a few weeks out. Weekends are best—Saturdays first, Fridays second, and Sundays third. Steer clear of weekdays, holiday weeks, and any time close to April 15, when people are worrying about paying their taxes. You might as well start in the early morning. That's when people are going to show up anyway.
- *Go through your house and decide what goes.* A good rule of thumb: If you haven't used it in two years, you can live without it. But don't throw anything away. Even if you think it's junk, someone else collects it.
- *Treat your sale like a business.* Organize the merchandise, putting like with like, so buyers can find what they're looking for. If you're selling clothing, put it on a rack, or string up a clothesline and hang it for people to see.
- *Advertise.* Run ads in local papers and on the Internet (there are lots of free yard- and garage-sale sites), and put up flyers. Be specific about what sort of merchandise you have—clothing, antiques, whatever. You'll get the people who really want that stuff.

continued

- *Spend time on your signs.* Much garage-sale traffic just follows the signs, so make sure you write in large, legible block print on sizable, strong oak tag or foam core. Make your directions clear ("1/4 mile on left"). Then take your signs down after the sale is over so your neighbors won't get annoyed.

- *Consider joining forces.* In the world of garage sales, more is better. If you're not sure you have enough to fill your yard, collaborate with a few families. To keep track of who's earned what, put different-colored price tags on each family's items. Then make sure whoever's minding the register knows the code.

- *Be prepared to haggle.* Keep that in mind as you attach price tags to your merchandise. If you're firm on a particular item, write that on the tag as well, as in "$75 firm." If you see that items aren't going at their original prices, drop prices throughout the day to get rid of as much as you can.

- *Don't forget to . . .* Check with your town or village to see if you need a permit (you might). Mark your house clearly with balloons or signs, as if you were having a birthday party. Don't take checks. Have plenty of change and small bills on hand, as well as old grocery bags and newspaper for wrapping. Post a sign near the register that reads ALL SALES FINAL. And on a hot day, sell cold sodas for $1 a can. That should substantially boost your take.

- *Donate anything that's left.* Stuff that remains can be given to the Salvation Army, Goodwill, Big Brothers Big Sisters, or another local organization. You can take a tax deduction for the fair market value on this year's return. If you don't know what something's worth, consult the Goodwill Web site (goodwill.org) or eBay to see what like items are selling for. You can also go to itsdeductible.com, a free Web site that is part of the TurboTax system, to keep track of your deductions and see what your old stuff is worth.

Earning More

I know—you work hard already. But sometimes the only way to dig out is by earning extra money. You may be able to do that on your own job. If it's been a year or more since you've received a raise and your company is thriving rather than struggling, it's time to ask for one. If you don't get it, ask your supervisor what you need to do to increase the size of your pay-check.

If that doesn't work, you may need to get a second job. According to the Bureau of Labor Statistics, nearly eight million people held more than one job in the spring of 2009, an increase of nearly 300,000 since the recession of 2001. Many do so to meet regular household expenses or pay off debt. Branching out isn't just useful for your bank balance—it's good for your career not to have all your eggs in a single employer's basket.

There are certainly some primary jobs that are more moonlighting–friendly than others. BLS statistics show that the workers who moonlight most often (generally because of flexible work hours) are firefighters, physicians' assistants, announcers/disk jockeys/broadcasters, specialty artists and performers (such as calligraphers and circus clowns), and therapists and marriage counselors. The general rule if you're considering moonlighting is to clear it with your primary employer. Many companies don't have written policies on the practice, but whether or not yours does, you don't want to cause tension with the employer that's providing you (and perhaps your family) with health insurance. There may be something your current employer can do to increase your income, whether it's increasing your hours or your responsibilities. But you'll never know unless you ask.

Looking for a second job is much like looking for a first. Read want ads and surf job boards, but be sure to check out temporary services as well. Although unemployment has recently hit twenty-five-year highs, direct selling is an area that has continued to prosper, and temporary hiring continues to show gains. Temp services don't just place people from nine to five, either—they cut across all occupations and around the clock. If you're a temp, you don't have to worry that you'll let someone down once your financial situation has improved and you're ready to leave. You can also try to match your skills with other areas of the economy poised to grow: health care, education, and alternative energy, to name three.

Tales of Life and Debt: Kitty

For four years in the late 1990s, Kitty, a thirty-six-year-old office manager, was married to a man who was a financial fiasco. More to the point, he just didn't have a clue about the toll debt could take. Her new hubby came out of law school with $120,000 in student loans and promptly decided he didn't want to be an attorney. Both of them had jobs, but they found it tough to live below their means. Kitty's husband spent more than he earned on toys and other gadgets. He took on a $25,000 car loan. He'd often charge on her credit card without her permission, Kitty recalls.

She could have handled all of that. What she couldn't handle was that when she tried to talk to him about his spending problem, he wasn't willing. "He wouldn't sit down with me to figure out how to get out of this mess," she says. In the end, she decided she couldn't live with someone so financially incompatible with her. So she left, leaving him with the student loans and taking the rest of the debt on her shoulders. She started a new life in Alaska.

Kitty knew that if she wanted to have a financial future, this time around it would have to be different. So she took the first job she was offered—waiting on tables in the morning and busing tables into the night. It wasn't glamorous, but it was lucrative. She kept spending to a minimum. "I shopped sales, packed lunches, didn't dine out much, didn't buy a lot of clothes," she acknowledges. The process worked. She cleared the credit card debt. Within a year, she was able to pay off her car.

By 2001, she'd had enough of the restaurant life and found an office job. Even though the debt was gone, she continued to live a frugal lifestyle that enabled her to start saving. "I never used to have savings—ever," she says. "We always lived paycheck to paycheck." But she found that having money in the bank gave her a level of comfort, a feeling of stability.

It also enabled her to buy a home. Kitty saved $10,000 for a down payment and bought a $171,000 fixer-upper in the city of Juneau in the summer of 2003. She got an interest rate of 5.25 percent—an affirmation of the fact that her credit score was excellent. Then she went about furnishing the place via her local thrift stores. "I couldn't afford to buy new," she says. "Even a cheap bedroom set in Juneau is about $1,500 [new], because everything has to be brought in on a truck. I probably spent a total of $1,000—on everything. And it's really cute, really nicely furnished."

She didn't stop there. She quickly socked away $1,000 in savings in the bank in case of emergencies and opened lines of credit in the event the savings account was insufficient. In 2004, she opened an IRA with a substantial deposit. She's managed to make room to spend money on the things that she really enjoys—such as Lancôme cosmetics and expensive cologne. And her feeling of security has continued to grow.

The best part is that these days she sleeps really well at night. "I didn't sleep for six months during my divorce. I lost thirty-three pounds, and it was extremely stressful," she says. "But now things are going along fine. I feel good because I have a backup plan for everything."

Tales of Life and Debt: Dan and Sarah

Dan and Sarah were both liberal-arts students. He wanted to be a poet; she wanted to run a restaurant. "I guess like spirits do attract," Dan muses. Both came out of graduate school with a heap of student-loan and credit card debt. So they moved to Boston, found the cheapest apartment possible, and tried to live on their all-too-small entry-level salaries. He was thirty years old, making $23,500 at a public-relations firm. ("I made more as a bellhop at the University of Virginia," he gripes.) She was a few years younger, managing a restaurant and making even less.

"We were kind of spinning our wheels for a few years, financially," he recalls. The money came in. The money went out. Both self-admitted food-and-wine geeks, they consumed more of it in restaurants than many people might have. But they believed life was meant to be enjoyed. Then one day they took stock. Dan, in particular, saw his fortieth birthday closing in. They wanted to buy a house—sooner rather than later. They wanted to have a baby. They decided to change their financial lives. "We knew that if we didn't come up with some sort of plan, we could waste another five or ten years and nothing would happen. We might have had better jobs and better pay, but we still would have had the same financial problems."

So they mustered their courage. "It was hard," says Dan. They made an appointment with a financial planner, who put together an initial plan to guide them on the path to reducing their debts and starting to save. The first few steps were very basic. They called their credit card companies and asked for a reduction in their interest rates. Their Discover card lender dropped the rate from 18 percent down to less than 10 percent. "That was the easiest thing to do," says Dan. "It gave us enough quick gratification that we knew that we could actually make a dent in this thing." They made some small adjustments in their spending: Sarah stopped buying clothes for a while; eating out became a special occasion, not an everyday occurrence.

But the other steps they took—and choices they made—were much harder. They decided to live without a car. Walking to work and traveling longer distances via public transportation saved them thousands of dollars a year. They decided they needed to make more money. Dan took a look at his field—high-tech PR—and he could see that there was a growth curve in the industry and in his company. He believed that if he put in his time, there was an opportunity to prosper. But not for Sarah. So she switched careers, taking a page from her husband's book and pursuing a job doing PR for a software company.

After working extra hard, including weekends, to

outperform expectations on the job, Dan and Sarah started to put some serious money away. As they were digging out of debt, both became avid participants in their companies' 401(k) plans. They were able to achieve every one of their goals. Fast-forward: Dan and Sarah own a house in the Boston suburbs and they have a beautiful family. "It all came together in a pretty powerful way," he says.

STEP 9

Pay It Down—Intelligently

—◆—

Who Gets Paid First?

When it comes to paying off your credit cards, there's only one basic rule: Pay the highest interest rates first. I know there are differing opinions on this. Some people say you should pay off the smallest debt to get rid of one card faster. I've heard others say that when you get a great balance-transfer offer, you should start paying on that card so that you make headway while you have access to those low interest rates.

Both are wrong. You pay off your highest-rate debts first because those are the ones that are costing you the most. Let's say you have three credit cards and you owe a total of $9,500:

Card A: $5,000 at 12 percent
Card B: $1,500 at 16 percent
Card C: $3,000 at 24 percent

The minimum payment on each card is 2 percent of the outstanding balance. How much do you save by paying them off in order of highest interest rate rather than highest balance or lowest balance?

Let's assume you can come up with another $200 a month—above your minimums—to put toward your balance, so you'll write checks totaling $390.

If you pay as much as you can toward the card with the highest interest rate, and pay the minimums on the others, you'll pay a total of $1,818.69 in interest.

If you pay as much as you can toward the card with the lowest balance and pay the minimums on the others, you'll pay a total of $1,969.19 in interest.

And if you pay as much as you can toward the card with the highest balance and pay the minimums on the others, you'll pay a total of $2,517.34 in interest.

In other words, by doing it the right way, you'll save $700. And that's truly impressive.

So, lay all your cards out on the table. Note the interest rate you're paying on each one; that'll tell you where to put your muscle in terms of paying them off.

(*Note:* As you pay down the first card, your minimum payment will decrease. Your goal under the $10-a-day plan has been to pay what you were paying before [the minimum] plus an extra $10 a day, or $304 a month, but if you maintain the minimum payments you started with and *then* add your $304 a month, you'll get out of the debt hole even faster.)

What If You Can't Pay Everyone?

Then there's this problem: What if you're trying to put away your $10 a day to pay off your bills and build some savings—and you hit a bump in the road? It happens. What are you supposed to do if there's a month or two when you simply don't have the money to pay everyone? Follow these rules:

Necessities first. These are the things you absolutely need to live. You need your house, so it's important to pay the mortgage or the rent. You need it to be warm in the winter and lit year-round, so it's key to pay the utility company. You need a phone, so Ma Bell gets paid. You need transportation to work, so you make the car payment. If you owe child support, it's a must-pay not only because that's part of being a good parent, but because not paying can get you thrown in jail. You need some cash—your emergency cushion—so that you won't have to accumulate more debt if you need (yes, need) to spend some money unexpectedly. And finally, because getting in to see the doctor these days—particularly if you have no health insurance—requires paying the bill then and there, you need to take care of medical emergencies.

Uncle Sam second. If you don't have the money to pay your taxes immediately, the IRS will generally work with you to come up with a schedule of payments. By all means, though, file your taxes when they are due. Not filing at all, or even filing late, can result in penalties and interest of up to 25 percent of what you owe.

Most student loans are backed by the government. That means that, like back taxes, the government is allowed to come after these loans in ways that other creditors aren't. If you're delinquent in paying your back taxes or student loans, the government can seize your tax refunds and garnishee your wages and, in some cases, your Social Security benefits. Fortunately, the government also has a number of solutions for people who can't afford to make their student-loan payments, including putting those loans on hold if you're out of work, or stretching out the repayment term of the loan and thereby reducing the amount owed each month.

Everything else third. All of your other debts—bank-card debts, department-store debts, payments for furniture and appliances—are back-burner debts. That doesn't mean you shouldn't pay them. You borrowed the money; of course you should try to pay them. But if you're in a situation in which you know that not every creditor is going to get paid, these are the ones you put on hold.

Once you fall behind on payments, what—gulp!—is likely to happen next? Your creditors will start to call. After a month or so, you'll get a letter demanding payment. At this point, you have a decision to make. If you're in a temporary financial slump, one you can see ending in the next couple of months, it's worth calling those creditors and explaining the situation to see if you can put a halt to the collection process and negotiate better terms for paying back what you owe. But part of the deal will likely be agreeing not to charge any more on your card.

If you can see from where you're sitting that your situation is more long term than temporary, you should know that somewhere in the next three to six months—after you've been ninety days late—your creditor is going to turn over your file to a collection agency. Your credit card company may have called once or twice to try to nudge you to pay, but it's when you become a prospect for a collection agency that the calls begin in earnest. You're now dealing with people who are paid a commission of one third to one half of any money they can get you to ante up to your credit card company. That's why they're so relentless.

But just because they're the loudest, it doesn't mean that they should be paid first—or even second or third. Even though they call you day and night, your priorities are still your true needs and government-related obligations. Why? Because other than damaging your credit rating and your credit score (not the best scenario in the world, but also not the worst), there's very little these lenders can do to you. There's no collateral behind the money you owe them. There's nothing they can even try to take from you. They went into business with you—lending you more money than perhaps you could pay back—knowing that. They made a calculated bet on you. They knew they were going to lose a certain amount of money each year on clients who, when push came to shove, couldn't afford to pay. For now, it's their loss.

Once you've found your $10 (or more) each month and decided where it's going, the challenge becomes getting that money out of your hands and into the hands of your creditors, your savings account, or your brokerage account before you have the chance to spend it.

You can try to do this yourself, but I wouldn't. If you're sixty or more days late to a credit card company, you can see a relatively sane interest rate soar into the mid-20-percent range—or higher. By far the best way to be sure that your money gets where you want it to go is to use some form of automatic transfer.

The good news is that moving money around automatically is now easier and cheaper than it's ever been. It's tough to find a financial-services provider that *doesn't* offer you some way to do this. They're not fools. They've read the writing on the wall and it says that automatic payments aren't only the wave of the future; they're the wave of the present. Americans already make more payments automatically—by credit card and debit card in addition to electronic bill payment—than with checks. And that number is growing fast.

Consumers have caught on to the fact that automatic transfers are hugely convenient. According to findings from Javelin Strategy and Research, it takes an American household about two hours to pay by hand the ten to twelve bills it receives each month. Automating everything (after the setup) can cut that down to about fifteen minutes a month. That's why even people who begin by paying only a couple of bills electronically are soon paying them all that way.

Let's talk about how this would work in practice. You go to work and earn a paycheck. That paycheck gets deposited (direct-deposited, preferably) into your checking account. You know you want that money to go toward repaying, say, your highest-rate Visa bill. Because you're no longer racking up new charges on that card, you know about what you'll be paying on it—the minimum plus the additional $10 a day. Now you can schedule an automatic transfer into that account on a date that's convenient for you (perhaps right after you receive a paycheck) but before the bill is due. And you can schedule minimum payments for the rest of your cards, your mortgage, your car loan, and any other bill you pay regularly.

You can do this, as I do, through your bank. Most offer bill-payment services, and many, because they're so eager to have customers switch to electronic bill payment (cheaper for the bank than processing checks), offer it for free. If you want in on this party, it's important to understand that you're not locked in to bill payment only through your bank—though for many people that sort of consolidation makes sense. Here's a look at your electronic–payment options, and their natural fit:

Direct-debiting. By far the easiest solution, direct-debiting is a process in which you authorize one of your creditors to reach its electronic fingers into your checking account and pull out a certain amount of money every month. In practice it works best when the payment is fixed, as it is with your mortgage, health–club dues, car payment, even utilities (whereby you balance your bills every month for consistency, then settle up at the end of the year). If you're not ready to go fully online but want to take a step in that direction, start here. The downside: If your balance isn't fat enough to cover these withdrawals, you'll get hit with late and over–limit fees. Once you have paid back your creditors and are moving money into a savings or brokerage account instead, this is how you'll schedule deposits into those accounts. You'll authorize your bank or brokerage firm to pull out the money before you have the opportunity to spend it.

Biller-direct payment. Many credit card companies and other big billers allow you to go to their Web sites and pay your bill. It requires some setup—you generally need a user ID and password—but after that it's very easy. You can see your current statement online, as well as other recent transactions, and you can choose how much you want to pay, from the minimum to the entire balance. Print a receipt for yourself, and you're done. One of the big benefits is that this is something you can do down to the wire. In many cases, the payment can be posted the day you make it (though sometimes billers charge for this). If you go through a bank, it takes a couple of days. By coupling biller-direct with direct-debiting, you can sizably reduce the number of checks you write without fully automating. The downside: You have to travel from site to site to pay your bills.

One-stop bill payment. Your other option—and in my opinion the best option—is to pay your bills at a single site. You can do this through your bank, but there are other players in this market as well. The big benefit of one-stop bill payment (beyond the one-stop convenience) is that it will allow you to see your account balances before you write checks, and you'll be able to do everything from one site. The catch is that there's sometimes a fee of anywhere from about $7 to $11 a month. That's particularly true with the third-party sites. Many banks, however, have made it free for everyone.

Once you pick a solution, there's setup to contend with. If you're going the one-stop way, that means entering your account information and the name and address of the creditors and other billers you regularly pay. You can choose which day of the month each bill will be paid and which account you want the money to come from, and for bills that run the same amount month to month, you can even schedule payment in advance. The one caveat: You still have to keep a careful eye on due dates, or at least build in a buffer. Money doesn't move from your bank to your biller instantaneously. If your biller is set up to accept electronic payments (most companies are), it can take up to three days. If your biller isn't set up to accept electronic payments (many individuals aren't), your electronic bill payer will send a check through the mail, which can take five days before the money gets into their hands.

Finally, there's one other benefit of going high-tech, no matter how you do it: Just as filing your taxes electronically dramatically reduces the error rate, so does paying bills electronically. The fewer human hands touching your paperwork, the better. Still, it's your responsibility to be sure the proper amount of money has been transferred or withdrawn.

What if you're a technophobe? What if the thought of all these electronic transfers gives you the heebie-jeebies? You know you can trust yourself—once you've freed up all that money—to parse it out by check. The old-fashioned solution is fine as long as you stay on your toes. It's a good bet the same folks who never—*ever*—use ATMs (yes, they exist) prefer to pay their bills by hand as well. Just set up a series of reminders for yourself. Mark the dates your bills are due on every calendar in the house. If you use an electronic organizer or calendar program, schedule pop-ups to prompt you to pay as well.

STEP 10

How to Deal When Things Go Wrong

⌐◆⌐

There may be times along this road to wealth when things go wrong. It's my wish for everyone who picks up this book that they'll find their $10 a day, put it to work for them, and be able to stop worrying (at least about their money) forever. But I'm enough of a realist to know that although I can wish it, it's not going to happen for everyone.

Some people will suffer the same sorts of bumps in the road that got them into debt to begin with: health scares, divorces, unemployment, spending that's beyond their control. If you're one of the people who find themselves in deep trouble, I want you to have the information and resources you need to handle it. Here's some advice to get you started on dealing with a shopping problem, creditors that won't stop calling, or a pending foreclosure of your home.

Do You Have a Shopping Problem?

Do you hide purchases—or receipts for purchases? Do you buy things in cash so your spouse won't notice? Do you get a craving if you haven't shopped in a while—and a high when you actually buy? Is every trip to the mall followed by feelings of guilt, then yet another round of cravings? Do you buy things to punish your spouse or the other people in your life?

If the answer to one or more of these questions is yes, then you may very well have a shopping addiction. The thing about a shopping problem, unlike a drinking problem or a drug problem, is that it's so easy to mask. Even highly addicted shoppers seem to be smart (they're certainly smart about getting a good deal), well-educated people—and they're participating in an activity that's completely acceptable. It's social. You can do it with your friends.

How do you deal with a shopping problem? As you do with any other addiction—by getting help. There are therapists who specialize in dealing with financial issues. Marriage/couples therapists tend to be particularly strong in this area because money problems are such a big threat to relationships. Some antidepressants have proven to be effective in dealing with shopping disorders. There are also twelve-step programs, run by not-for-profits such as Debtors Anonymous as well as for-profit therapists, that can help you deal with the underlying causes of your shopping/debt problem and give you the support you need to get through. You can find a Debtors Anonymous group near you on the Internet at debtorsanonymous.org.

When You Need Credit Counseling

What if you've made it through this book and you still can't make ends meet? You've tried to reduce your interest rates, find extra money, sell assets, get a second job . . . and it's just not working. It's time to consider other solutions. Credit counseling is one of them.

Credit counselors use a formalized approach to debt collection. They work by putting clients—for whom they decide it is appropriate—on a debt-management program, or DMP. If you are accepted into a DMP, your credit counselors will arrange for you to pay off your debts at lower interest rates. (How much of a break they are able to net you varies by creditor, not by counselor or client. Card issuers have a schedule of the breaks they're willing to give to counselors and they don't vary from that schedule.) If you go into a DMP, late fees and other penalties you've assessed will also be waived, which for many clients can be more of a relief than the interest-rate break.

In exchange, you will agree to stop using your cards and not to apply for additional credit. From this point on, rather than writing checks each month to your creditors, you'll make one payment each month (usually electronically) to your counseling firm. The counselor will, in turn, distribute the money to the creditors you owe. For doing this, your creditors will rebate a portion of the money (known in the industry as a "fair-share contribution") to your counseling firm. But DMPs aren't free to you, either. You'll pay both a monthly and an up-front fee.

How do you know whether you should consider counseling? You should if you:

- Are using one credit card to pay off another
- Are taking out cash advances because you don't have cash

- Have asked for an increase in your credit line and been denied
- Have lost track of how much debt you have
- Are using your credit cards to pay for groceries because you don't have the money
- Are worrying about money constantly

Unfortunately, credit counseling is a field—like many others—in which you can't trust every person or group that advertises that it can help you. Several years ago, we went through a period in which some large and prominent credit counselors were investigated by the Federal Trade Commission, sued by various attorneys general, and called before Congress to testify. You don't need to worry about the minutiae as much as you need to understand this: You can't assume every credit-counseling group is good. You have to look at each one individually, check it out, and make a decision about whether or not you believe it can help you.

How do you know if a counseling organization is credible? Having not-for-profit status is a good start, but it's not enough. So:

- Look in the Yellow Pages to see that the organization is recognized by the Better Business Bureau.

- Call the Better Business Bureau to be sure there's no history of consumer complaints.
- Ask the organization if it's a member of the National Foundation for Credit Counseling (NFCC) or the Association of Independent Consumer Credit Counseling Agencies. Both use only certified credit counselors.

When you've narrowed your list, ask the counselors these questions to make your final decision:

Ask: What do you do?

Bad answer: We consolidate debts or put people on debt-management plans.

Good answer: We'll evaluate your financial situation to see what sort of solution is right for you. The counselor can't know whether your finances are appropriate for a DMP until he or she has been through them. Your situation might be good enough that you can work through it on your own—or so bad that a DMP won't help and you need a bankruptcy attorney.

Ask: How much time will you spend with me in an initial consultation?

Bad answer: Less than half an hour.

Good answer: A half hour or more. [It's impossible to figure much out in less than a half hour. An hour is even better.]

Ask: What kind of debt do you help people with?

Bad answer: Just credit card debt.

Good answer: All kinds of debt; we even have a housing counselor on staff who can help you deal with your mortgage. You don't just want a counselor to deal with your credit cards if your car loan, student loan, and mortgage are causing you worry as well.

Ask: Can I come see you in person?

Bad answer: No, we only work over the phone.

Good answer: Absolutely. We have an office where we can meet with you and go over your paperwork. Sitting down face-to-face is, in my opinion, often more effective.

Ask: How much will this cost?

Bad answer: More than $75 up front. More than $35 a month.

Good answer: Less than $75 up front. Our monthly payments are on a sliding scale, but you won't pay more than $35 a month.

The Lowdown on Debt Settlement

Debt–settlement companies work as a middleman be-tween you and your creditor. If all goes well (that's a big *if*), you should be able to settle your debts for cents on the dollar. You'll also pay a fee to the debt–settlement company, usually either a percentage of the total debt you have or a percentage of the total amount for-given.

If you'd asked me a few years ago about debt-settlement companies, I probably would have told you to avoid them at all costs. I'm still not a fan. As I write this, Andrew Cuomo, the Attorney General of New York State, has just launched a major investigation of com-panies in this industry, accusing them of fraud. But I do have to acknowledge that there are good eggs in this industry as well as bad ones. So now my advice is to avoid them until you have tried all the other options—including settling your debts yourself. If you're on your last legs, you may want to consider giving debt-settlement companies a try.

Here's how settlement generally works: The debt-settlement company will direct you to stop paying your creditor and instead send the money directly to them each month. The company's goal is to demonstrate to your creditor that you don't have the money to pay them—that's their leverage. After a few months, they typically go to the creditor and say, "I'm holding X dollars on behalf of your customer. He doesn't have the money to pay you, so you should take this amount as a settlement or you'll end up with nothing." If the creditor wants to get paid badly enough, they'll take the money.

It's not a system without its negatives. During the three- to four-month stretch that you're not paying your creditor, your account is racking up late fees, and possibly even over-limit fees. Both of those add to the total debt, and to the debt-settlement company's fee. Not paying your creditors can do a serious number on your credit score, and having a settlement on your history drags it down even further. If you start out in the high 600s, for example, your credit score could be well into the 400s by the time all is said and done, especially if you settle more than one account.

And here's a little-known fact: You really don't need to hire a debt-settlement company to negotiate with your creditors. Unless you have multiple accounts that you need to negotiate and you think the project is just too big to tackle on your own, you're better off just calling your creditors directly. Tell them how much you have to offer and ask them if they are willing to settle for that amount.

If you're considering going this route, make sure that any company you deal with is a member of The Association of Settlement Companies (TASC), a trade association that represents debt-settlement firms and outlines standards that they agree to meet. The association has a search tool on their Web site that allows you to find a registered member in your area. Once you've pinpointed a few viable choices, ask for an initial consultation. You should also, of course, make sure the company has a clean record with the Better Business Bureau, which you can do at bbb.org.

And there are a few red flags to beware of. First, the fee: It should be based on the amount of debt that they are able to settle for you. If the company charges a percentage of your total debt up front, walk away. Second, lack of a guarantee. There should be a money-back guarantee for at least thirty days after you sign up. Third, no timeline. No company can promise an end date, but if you have multiple debts, the first one should be settled within a year. Fourth and finally, a safe holding pen for your money. Once you send it to the debt-settlement company, it should be kept in an FDIC-insured bank account. If they ask you to keep it, or if they don't deposit it in an insured account, they aren't doing their job.

Dealing with Debt Collectors

Credit card delinquencies are at an all-time high. That's been good news for debt collectors because it means business is booming. It's expensive for corporations to try to chase you down on their own, so after a few (often cursory) in-house efforts, they hand your file over to a debt collector, who earns a certain percentage of whatever they can get you to pay in commission. Some debt collectors play purely by the rules, but others are cowboys who have little trouble pressuring you, antagonizing you, frightening you, calling you at all hours of the day or night—in fact, doing whatever they can to get you to pony up.

That's why complaints against debt collectors have been steadily rising. The Federal Trade Commission received nearly 79,000 complaints about debt collectors in 2008—an 11-percent increase over 2007. For context, that represented 19 percent of all of the complaints received by the FTC. Another measure of the steadily rising number of complaints: the number of lawyers in business to handle them. A decade ago there were two attorneys processing suits against collection agencies. Now, according to the National Consumer Law Center, there are more than one hundred.

How do you know if a debt collector calling you has gone too far? Generally you'll know it in your gut, but it helps tremendously if you understand what collectors are and are not allowed to do to get you to pay. According to the Fair Debt Collection Practices Act (FDCPA) of 1977, collection agencies are *not* allowed to:

- Call you before eight a.m. or after eight p.m.
- Use deceptive, unfair, or abusive practices when trying to collect their debts
- Threaten litigation (creditors have the right to sue; collectors don't)
- Lie to you by telling you they're going to throw you in jail or contact your boss
- Call you on the job if they know that it's not possible for you to take these calls at work (because you're a teacher, for example)
- Call you on the job if they know your employer has prohibited it
- Threaten to garnishee your wages (they can't do that unless they have a judgment)

Understanding those ground rules, what's the best way to deal with debt collectors?

Hang up the phone. You don't have to talk to collectors. And you don't have to return their calls. Many consumers make the mistake of trying to reason with debt collectors. If you know that what you're being called about is a debt you didn't accrue, call the credit-reporting agencies and get a copy of your credit report, which will help you to get to the root of the problem.

Ask the collector to cease contact. Make it clear to the person on the phone that you would work with him or her if you could, but right now you can't do that. Then ask the collector to cease contact because it is causing you distress. That's important, because when you tell collectors they're causing you distress, they are supposed to stop.

Put it in writing. Unfortunately, it's not enough to ask that a collector stop calling; you need proof that you did it. Taping the call is legal in some states—but not every state, so you're better off getting the name and address of the collection agency or creditor calling you, and writing to them. You can use the letter on page 189 or write your own. Again, the point is to ask them to stop calling because it causes you distress. Then send your letter via certified mail, return receipt requested. Collection agencies have to stop when they get such a letter. Creditors don't, but often if they get the feeling that you are truly upset, they'll start worrying about being sued for harassment, so they'll stop as well.

Get a lawyer. If you're being harassed, there are now a significant number of lawyers in this country who will represent you. Settlements aren't generally for a ton of money—they start at $2,000 or $3,000 and go up from there. That's because debt collectors know that unless you can prove you've been damaged by their actions— that you've lost a job, for example, or suffered a mental breakdown—the most you'll be awarded in court is $1,000 plus attorney fees and costs. But you can try. For a list of lawyers, try the National Association of Consumer Advocates Web site, naca.net.

Avoiding Foreclosure

Americans are having a tougher time than ever making their mortgage payments. In 2003, 1 percent of mortgages were in foreclosure. By 2004, that number had increased to a record 1.23 percent, representing 640,000 homes and the highest rate of foreclosures in thirty years of record keeping. By 2008, the number of

Letter to Collection Agency
to Cease and Desist

Date

Your name

Your address

City, state, zip

Name of person at collection agency

Collection–agency name

Address

City, state, zip

RE: [*insert account number*]

Dear [*name of agent or agency*]:

I am writing to request that you cease and desist in your efforts to collect on account number [*xxxx*], for [*$ amount of debt*]. I will resolve this matter with the original creditor, and do not want to be contacted further, by phone or mail, by a collection agency.

This is in compliance with the laws of the Fair Debt Collection Practices Act. If you fail to comply with this notice, I will file a formal complaint with the Federal Trade Commission as well as my state's Attorney General's office.

Sincerely,

[*Your signature*]

[*Your typed name*]

foreclosures had nearly quintupled—RealtyTrac logged 3.1 million total that year. And lest you think the number would come down, by the time I put pen to paper (or fingers to keyboard) to update *Pay It Down!* in mid-2009, another quarter-million homes were entering foreclosure every three months.

Nobody wins in a foreclosure. The borrower gets a bad credit record and the lender spends time and a lot of money—an average $2,500—going through this process. So if you are having trouble making your mortgage payments, you need to know what's on the road ahead. Miss three consecutive payments and a "breach letter" will arrive from your lender signaling you're in violation of your contract. You then have a month to respond. Let that month go by and the lender has the right to foreclose, which means they take ownership of the house.

Letting that three months slip past is the biggest mistake homeowners in trouble make. Instead, here are the steps you should follow:

Call your lender immediately. Explain why you're having difficulty making payments, how long that difficulty will last, and what will have to happen in order for the problem to be resolved. Be prepared to provide financial details, including monthly income and expenses.

The goal here is to get lenders on your side in helping you to solve your problem. So don't wait for the lender to call you. If you call them, they'll see that you're not trying to shirk your responsibility. If you don't feel able to talk to your lender and explain your situation yourself, a not-for-profit HUD housing counselor can help. Call 1-888-995-HOPE or go to hopenow.com to avail yourself of this free service.

Ask for partial payments. If you have an FHA loan, your lender may be willing to allow you to make a partial payment—$700, for example, instead of the full $1,000 you owe—for a short while without changing the terms of your mortgage. You generally can't do that with a conventional Fannie Mae or Freddie Mac loan. But if you call and say you've just missed a payment, your lender will generally tell you that you can make up that payment by spreading it over the next few months.

Refinance. If you have yet to miss a payment and you have a decent amount of equity in your home, refinancing can lower your payments in a number of ways. You can lower your interest rate, extend the term of your loan (thereby stretching out your payments), or convert some of the equity in your home to a cash cushion you could use to get by.

Look at a loan modification. If you don't have much

equity or you owe more than your home is worth—up to 105 percent of its appraised value—and your loan is guaranteed by Fannie Mae or Freddie Mac, you still may be able to qualify for a loan modification under President Obama's Making Home Affordable plan. This can lower your payments by reducing your interest rate and/or extending your term. For more information on this plan, turn to page 89 or go to makinghomeafford able.gov.

If, after you've considered all of these alternatives, staying in your house doesn't look possible, there are two fixes to consider. The first is called a "preforeclosure sale." It will allow you to sell your property (while living there) and move on in an organized fashion.

The second, prior to foreclosure, is something called a "short sale." Under the terms of a short sale, you make a deal with your lender that allows you to sell your home for less than the amount that you owe. The lender gets the money from the sale, while you get nothing, but you walk away and—in most cases—no longer owe the balance on the loan (sometimes the lender can make you cough up some of the difference, which is something you need to work out at the onset).

As you can probably imagine, it's not easy to get your lender to allow a short sale. But in 2008 and 2009 it wasn't impossible either. You'll have to convince your lender and that involves outlining your financial situation, with backup: paychecks, tax returns, credit card and bank statements. If you were laid off, you'll need a letter from your former employer. If you were divorced, you'll have to cough up the paperwork. If you're suffering from a medical emergency, be prepared to prove it. You should be controlling your spending—high credit card debt, particularly anything that was recently charged, can work against you, because if you're spending elsewhere, the lender will (justifiably) wonder why you can't afford your home.

To be clear: A short sale is not ideal for you or for the lender. It ranks one step above foreclosure, however, because it allows you to avoid the lengthy legal process that accompanies foreclosure, and it may look slightly better to future lenders because it shows that you were involved in this process, you talked to your lender, and you worked out a deal. These days lenders prefer short sales to an alternative called a "deed in lieu of foreclosure," which allows you to hand over the keys and the title of the home to the bank. You no longer have ownership of the home, and the bank should waive the balance of the loan. With a deed in lieu, your lender gets your house (and chances are lenders have more real estate than they want right now). With a short sale, your lender gets at least some cash, which is preferable.

Finally, if you owe mortgage debt and the amount is forgiven through a short sale, you'll owe taxes on that amount. The IRS treats it as taxable income. But the Mortgage Debt Relief Act of 2007 means that taxpayers can exclude income from debts forgiven on their principal residence in most cases. This act lasts through 2012, and includes up to $2 million of forgiven debt for singles or married couples filing jointly. (It caps at $1 million for married couples filing separately.)

Tales of Life and Debt: Recovering from a Setback

Chris, an entrepreneur based outside Atlanta, sent me this message. I couldn't tell his story better, so I decided to let him tell it himself:

> *My wife and I are responsible, hardworking, dedicated, and giving people. We both paid our way through school. It took me ten years to earn my degree. I joined the Navy reserves, used loans, and at times worked four jobs. We both graduated in 1994 and we still have $23,000 in student-loan debt.*

In 1995, I closed a business (a business I did not belong in) with about $160,000 in debt. We never declared bankruptcy and eventually paid back what we owed in 1998. Over the next few years, I focused on my career. It seemed that every two years, I took a better job and we would move.

In 1999, we ended up in Atlanta. We thought we had finally made it. I had a great job as operations director of a large hyperbaric medical center. And my wife got her first position as a kindergarten teacher for a private school. We bought a house, new cars, and had our first child. We started investing in our own retirement accounts and saved. We paid off our credit cards monthly. We were finally on track and trying to live within our means.

Toward the end of my first year, my employers were not living up to the contract we had, especially in the area of my bonus. This continued to be a problem, but I was reassured that it would be resolved. In February 2002, my employers tried to add to the contract they weren't honoring and I put my foot down. So they resolved the issues by firing me. To date they owe me about $35,000. I will never see it because it will cost too much to pursue.

Now we were off track again. I was collecting unemployment. My wife made $20,000. We had no health insurance, a *mortgage, bills, and a new baby boy. We lost most of our re-tirement account during the crash. Still, we took care of the necessities, including new health insurance. As a result we have racked up—to date—over $20,000 in credit card debt.*

I kept looking for a new job, but I was discouraged. After a few months, I told the unemployment counselor that I was going to start my own business placing and managing hy-perbaric medical services (a business that I do belong in). I wrote my own business plan, drained our emergency fund, acquired an SBA loan, and acquired a nine-year contract with a medical facility. The doors opened in January 2003 and we have been growing slowly and helping lots of people. I was able to pay myself a small salary after the sixth month.

So here we are in January 2004. I have been in busi-ness for one year, in which my company made over $100,000. I plan to double the business at the first facility and add two more facilities this year.

Right now all the bills are being paid at home and with the company. But they are far from being paid off. Our goals are to get rid of our personal credit card debt, increase our savings and retirement accounts, pay off our student loans, and save for college. This past weekend I received great news. My wife told me she is pregnant with our second child. We are very happy about this and it now motivates us to do more about our financial future.

Let's take a look at what happened in Chris's life. After a rocky start, he was making smooth financial progress—paying down his debt and saving for the future. Then he lost his job. Particularly over the last few years, that's been one of the biggest reasons Americans have gone deeper into debt (health problems and divorce are the other two).

But Chris didn't give up. He regrouped. He thought long and hard about his skills and how he could best use them to make enough money to dig his family out of its hole. Having done it once before, he knew that although it would take time—and very likely be difficult—it was possible. So he started, one step at a time. Now, nearly two years into the process, he's well on his way. He has even more faith in his ability to take care of his family of four, now and in the years to come. And I'm right there with him. This is a guy who knows that slow and steady progress wins the race every single time.

STEP 11

Staying Ahead of the Game

Y ou've made it—through the book and into the program. I'd like to be able to tell you that you're finished. You're not. Steering clear of debt and building wealth is a lifelong endeavor. And right now the key is keeping your head above water. There are a few very important habits you can adopt to stay out of debt. These habits are here to help you make the most of (i.e., actually enjoy) your newfound financial freedom without sinking back into some destructive behavior patterns. They're here to help you protect what you've built—because as you now understand, this sort of freedom is a luxury that not too many people enjoy—as well as to help you on your journey.

Staying Out of Debt

For the record, one more time: I don't think there's anything wrong or bad or evil about credit cards. I think they're a flexible spending tool that when used wisely can make paying for the things you need to buy in this life much easier and much more convenient. You know you're using them at least fairly wisely if you can adhere to these two golden rules for credit card customers:

- Always pay more than the minimum.
- Always pay on time. Remember: Just two late payments can send your interest rate soaring.

If, however, you occasionally have trouble with those two rules, or you find yourself sliding back toward that minimum-payment habit, it's time to find another means of paying for your purchases. Two suggestions include:

Debit cards. The use of debit cards has been growing steadily. More consumers today opt to pay with debit cards than with credit cards. Smart folks. Debit cards, which draw money out of your checking account whenever you make a purchase, don't allow you to overspend in the same way that credit cards do (particularly if you do as I advise and opt out of overdraft protection). In the scheme of things this is a huge advantage. Huge. Bigger than huge, in fact. Enormous.

But there are a few key differences between debit and credit that you should be aware of.

First, if you use debit, you lose the float. If you use a credit card, you generally have twenty to twenty-five days to pay the bill. During that time, the money is yours to use, not the merchant's. (*Note:* This may change for the worse under the new Credit Cardholders' Bill of Rights. Grace periods will no longer be set in stone. It's important to keep an eye on the ball; otherwise you'll end up paying interest you weren't planning to pay.) Use debit and the money is spent.

Second, you lose some of the safety. If a credit card is stolen, you cancel it, and while you're liable for the first $50 of purchases you didn't make, most card issuers are waiving that nowadays. If your debit card is stolen, a thief could clean out your checking account before you even realize what's happened. Yes, your bank will give you back the money—many have the same "zero-liability" policies that they offer on their credit cards—but it's generally a bigger hassle than canceling a credit card.

And third—a distant third—you lose the miles. Now,

I want to note: Miles are a good deal only for people who pay off their credit cards every month. And they're not as good a deal as they used to be. But as long as you have a card with a grace period during which you do not—I repeat *do not*—have to pay a dime in interest in order to reap those rewards, I'm generally in favor of miles programs. Compare the annual fee you're pay-ing on a rewards card to the actual dollar value of the annual rewards you're garnering to figure out if it makes financial sense for you.

Prepaid/stored-value cards. For some people debit cards don't offer enough protection from their desire to spend. Why? Because they allow you to spend every-thing that's in your checking account at the time—money you may need for other uses. Some even allow you to go overboard: The overdraft protection on your checking account kicks in to cover whatever amount you "borrow," and you're faced with fees and interest. Then you have two choices. You can waive the over-draft protection. Do this and if you swipe your card and don't have money in the account, your purchase will be denied. That may be embarrassing but it won't cost you a hefty fee. Or, try a prepaid or stored-value card instead. These look like credit cards and work like a combination credit/ATM card, but the limits of your spending are finite. You load the card with whatever amount of money you choose (some employers are starting to offer stored-value cards in lieu of all or part of your paycheck, a boon for people who don't have bank accounts) and spend it down. You can also use it to get cash from an ATM. When the money is gone, it's gone. But note: Using the cards isn't free. Fees run anywhere from $3 a month to about $6, but that might be a price worth paying if it's the only way to keep yourself in line.

Starting to Save: The Eleventh Dollar

The other key to staying ahead of the game is saving. You need a savings stash to keep from sliding back into debt. Think about it: You're moving along, putting aside your $10 a day, paying down your credit cards, making terrific progress. Then your dog gets a nasty double ear infection. Between trips to the vet and pricey medications, this ends up costing you close to $200. Where is that money going to come from?

Unless you have a stash of savings, you're going to put that amount on your credit card. And although you now know enough to put it on your lowest-rate credit card, that purchase is going to set you back. It's going to impede your progress. And it's going to make you feel rotten. That's why you need savings.

Phase two of this program—after you've used your $10 a day to pay off your credit cards—is to take that $10 a day and stash it in a safe place, the highest-paying money-market account you can find (go to bankrate .com to find today's best rates), until you've got a substantial emergency cushion. You want the equivalent of three to six months' living expenses. That's your protection. If you get laid off, if the dog gets ill, if your transmission dies, you'll be able to live and pay your bills without sliding back into credit card debt.

But what about during phase one—while you're still focusing your energy on paying down your credit cards? *You still need to save something.* So the question becomes: Where do you get that money? Here are a few suggestions.

Windfalls. There are times when money falls into your lap. You get a bonus, a small inheritance, a tax refund, a stimulus payment from the government. Put that money away. Don't spend it. Consider it a down payment on whatever emergencies come later.

Raises. If and when you get a raise—even if it's just a few dollars per paycheck more than you were making previously—don't spend that money, either. Arrange a direct transfer of the precise amount of additional cash that's showing up in your paycheck from checking and into savings. Think about it logically: You were living without that cash before. If you start spending it immediately, it will be no time (I promise) before you can't remember how you ever lived on less. But if you pretend it's not there, you can use this raise to help your savings grow.

The eleventh dollar. Many of you, when you went through the process of finding money, ended up with a number bigger than $10 on the bottom line. I know $10 is what we were reaching for. But if you got to $11 or $12 or $15 or $20, I don't want you to put the excess toward your debt until you've accumulated your cash cushion. Again, arrange for a direct transfer of whatever additional money you found into savings. If you hit $10 on the nose, I want you to go back and find *one more dollar a day*. That's $365 a year to bail you out of a jam. What if you drew blood the last time around and feel you simply can't go back to the well? Then put this savings cushion together the old-fashioned way: with cash. Every day, take a dollar out of your wallet and put it into an emergency fund. Better yet, take your dollar and your change. I promise you, you won't miss it. And when Fido starts scratching his ears uncontrollably, you'll be very glad it's there.

Protect Yourself from Disaster with Health and Disability Insurance

There are two other things that could sabotage your ability to stay ahead of the game: a health scare and disability. As you work toward financial independence, it's important to insure yourself against both of these possibilities. They may never become realities—I hope in your case that they don't—but the point is, you can't know. And unless you're protected, either one of these scenarios can ruin you, not just in the short term but for years to come. Here's how to buy both in the most cost-efficient way.

Health insurance. The leading cause of personal bankruptcy is not wasteful spending or reckless investing but unpaid medical bills. That's surprising, but only until you consider that at any moment some 45 million Americans are without health insurance and another 40 million have experienced a gap in coverage sometime over the past two years. If you are laid off and you worked for a company with more than twenty employees, you can, by law, maintain your health coverage through your former employer's plan under a law called COBRA (the Consolidated Omnibus Budget

Reconciliation Act). The government is helping with those premiums—at least for now—but at an average of nearly $1,300 a month for families (eating up, by the way, 84 percent of the average unemployment check, according to recent reports) it's also a killing expense. The good news is, if you're in reasonably good health it's getting easier to find affordable health insurance on your own—particularly online.

You'll want to start on the Web, where, according to online-market leader ehealthinsurance.com, a healthy family of four (thirtysomething parents and school-age kids) can get a major medical plan—with a $1,000 annual family deductible and copayments of $35 per doctor's visit and $15 for generic drugs—for about $418 a month. The price falls to $221 a month with a $5,000 deductible. A healthy thirty-year-old single male can pay about $126 a month, or $60 with the higher deductible. Except in the states of New York, New Jersey, Massachusetts, Maine, and Vermont, you'll have to go through medical underwriting, answering health questions and opening up your medical records. (In most cases the insurance company, not the applicant, will obtain necessary medical records.) Depending on what's there, an insurer may want to charge a higher rate or exclude existing conditions. In such cases, COBRAing might be a better deal.

If you think that within the next six to twelve months you'll be back in the workforce, think about a short-term policy. Short-term policies are cheaper because they exclude coverage for existing medical conditions and reimburse a smaller percentage of your costs. The Web can lead you in the right direction there, as well.

Before you buy anything you find on the Web, however, you'll want to get a second opinion. So take your Web quotes to an insurance agent who can assess your needs, explain complex policy riders, and sometimes get you a better deal. You can search for agents in your area through the National Association of Health Underwriters, at nahu.org, although some insurers aren't in online databases. You want one who specializes in selling coverage to individuals.

Check out association coverage. Many institutional and professional groups, including alumni associations, offer well-priced coverage to members. But don't assume that your group has chosen a good company. Before signing up with any insurer, see whether its customers lodge a lot of complaints: Click on the "Consumer Information Source" link at naic.org, the National Association of Insurance Commissioners site. Check quality ratings at ncqa.org, the National Committee for Quality Assurance site. And before using an insurer based out of state, ask your state's insurance department whether you'll be protected if the company tries to raise your premium but not those of other policyholders.

Finally, consider a health savings account. These started rolling out onto the market in 2003. What do you need to know to understand if one might be right for you?

- *How they work.* HSAs are a little like IRAs. You buy a qualified health-insurance policy with a minimum deductible of $1,150 for singles and $2,300 for families. (In 2009, those numbers are indexed for inflation.) That enables you to open a health savings account, into which you can deposit pretax dollars up to the level of your deductible each year (capped in 2009 at $3,000 for individuals and $5,950 for families; there is no minimum). You don't have to deposit a lump sum all at once. Generally, you'll be able to make monthly deposits by automatic debit. Once the money is in the account, it's yours to spend—tax-free—on health care. If you don't use it, your money can remain in the account and grow tax deferred. (We'll get to your investment choices in a moment.) That gives HSAs a leg up on flexible-spending accounts (FSAs), in which you lose any

funds you don't use within the year. If you withdraw money from an HSA before you reach age
sixty-five for things other than IRS-approved
health-care expenditures, your withdrawals will be
taxed as income and you'll pay a 10-percent penalty. Once you hit 65, the penalty vanishes. At all
times, though, the money in the account belongs to
you. If you change jobs, you can take it with you.

- *What kind of health insurance you'll get.* So far, most HSAs
  are set up with preferred-provider organizations
  (PPOs), which offer you discounted rates on a network of physicians and hospitals until you reach
  your deductible, and cover 80 to 100 percent of in-
  network bills after that. These are basic policies,
  with some limitations on coverage.

- *How you open one.* According to a 2008 study by
  America's Health Insurance Plans, 6.1 million Americans are covered by HSA-qualified plans, including
  4.6 million through their employer. In fact, somewhere between one quarter and one third of all new
  health-insurance purchases among individuals and
  people who work for small employers are going this
  way. If your employer offers this option, someone in
  the HR or benefits department should be able to
  walk you through the process. If you're on your

own, a good place to start looking for a policy is, again, ehealthinsurance.com.

• *How you pick a good one.* Shop around, paying particular attention to how easy it is to access your money. Plans that come with checkbooks or debit cards are easier to administer than those that make you file paperwork to get reimbursed. The other deciding factor: your investment options. Some plans offer a fixed return on any money you deposit into the account. Others allow you to invest the money in a menu of mutual funds, stocks, bonds, or CDs. Whether you want to put your health-care dollars at risk depends on whether you have other reserves.

• *Bottom line.* If you already have a high-deductible individual policy, adding an HSA is a no-brainer for the tax savings alone. Otherwise, it may be a good bet if you're basically in good health. You should consider one if you've been paying more for health-insurance premiums than you've been using in care.

Disability insurance. Your chances of becoming disabled before you reach age sixty-five are six times as great as your chances of dying. Disability insurance is particularly important for single people who have no one else's income to fall back on. If you're single and you get injured and are unable to work, there will be no money coming in to pay your bills unless you've planned ahead and gotten this coverage. (To find the money, if you're single and paying for life insurance, cancel it. Singles who don't have dependents relying on them for financial support *do not need* life insurance.)

What's the most cost-effective way to purchase this coverage? Through your employer. Most company policies will get you only a portion of the coverage you need, however.

Optimally, a disability policy should replace 60 to 70 percent of your current income. Payment should kick in if you're unable to work in your own occupation, rather than just any occupation. This is really important. Say you're a surgeon and you injure your hand. You're now unable to perform your own high-paying job. But unless you have own-occupation coverage, the insurer may be able to make a case that you could work in a job that doesn't require such dexterity (maybe on the register line of a fast-food joint) and certainly won't pay as much. Other benefits, such as inflation protection, are less important.

Disability insurance isn't inexpensive. But you can bring the cost down by extending the waiting period between the time you become injured and the time coverage kicks in. Extending the waiting period from the standard thirty days to ninety days can mean a significant reduction in price. You can shop for disability insurance on the Internet, but you should also talk to an agent who specializes in these policies. Get at least three quotes from top-rated insurers before you buy.

Protect the You Everybody Else Sees: Monitor Your Credit Report

Since December 2004 every consumer has been entitled to receive one credit report free from each of the major credit bureaus (Equifax, Experian, and Trans-Union) per year. To get yours, go to annualcreditreport .com. You can get them all at once, but I'd suggest pulling one every four months. That way, you'll not only be able to see that your credit is holding up; you'll be able to tell if you've been a victim of identity theft.

In fact, checking your credit report is the *very best* free way to be sure you haven't been a victim of identity theft (more about that on page 217). If you have, your report will often show credit cards and loans that have been taken out in your name but don't belong to you. It's also key to check your credit three to six months before you apply for a mortgage or a car loan. This gives you a chance to clear up any misinformation before the lender pulls your credit report and score. If you've been lax about paying your bills, the three- to six-month window also gives you an opportunity to show the creditor that you've turned the situation around.

Here are the addresses, phone numbers, and Web sites of the three major credit bureaus, as well as FICO, where you can pull all three. Again, if you're going to pull only one, pull the one that's likely to give you the fullest file: Equifax in the South and Southeast, Trans-Union in the North and Northeast, and Experian in the West.

TransUnion
2 Baldwin Place
P.O. Box 2000
Chester, PA 19022
800-888-4213
tuc.com

Equifax
P.O. Box 740241
Atlanta, GA 30374
800-685-1111
equifax.com

Experian
P.O. Box 949
Allen, TX 75013
888-397-3742
experian.com

What to Look for on Your Credit Report

A study from U.S. Public Interest Research Group showed that 70 percent of credit reports—nearly three quarters!—have at least one error. The first time I pulled my report I found a doozy on it. The bureau had included information on my report from another Jean Sherman (my maiden name) who lived in Brooklyn (as I did at the time). Except this Jean Sherman had a lien on her house. It was curious to me that an error like this could be made—as an editorial assistant earning about $13,000 a year, I could hardly afford a house at the time. The silver lining is that most of these errors are not the sort that put someone else's lien on your report. They tend to be more administrative.

That's why, as you go through your report, you should pay particular attention to:

- Your identifying details, including name, Social Security number, and date of birth

- Addresses, current and former
- Employers, current and former
- Accounts: Are the correct ones listed as active and closed?
- Records of late payments
- Bankruptcies (which must be removed from your record after ten years), suits, judgments, tax liens, and arrest records (which must be removed after seven years)

How Do You Dispute Information on Your Credit Report?

Back when I found the problem on my credit report, I had no choice but to correct the information *sloooowwwly,* by snail mail. Today you can dispute information on your credit report online. The Web sites of all of the bureaus have instructions that take you through the process. If you're not comfortable online, you can use the letter on page 221 as a form letter.

What If the Bureau Won't Remove the Information?

If after investigating your claim the credit bureau agrees with you that the information is incorrect, it must remove the information and then send you a copy of the accurate report. If the credit bureau doesn't agree that the information should be removed, you can write a letter—or use the one I've provided (see page 222)—explaining your version of events and asking that the credit bureau attach it whenever your credit report is pulled. Until the matter is settled, a creditor can't give out information that would hurt your credit standing with potential creditors or other credit bureaus.

How Can You Protect Your Identity?

The truth is that it's very hard to completely shield your identity from thieves. I don't want to give you a false sense of security, because no matter what you do, you're always vulnerable. That's actually one of the first things that the Federal Trade Commission (FTC) tells people when they are asked this question.

That said, there are steps you can take to limit your exposure to identity theft, and luckily most of them are fairly easy and cheap, if not altogether free. Here's a run-through:

• Maintain control over your information. That means shredding documents before you put them in the trash. You can get a good crosscut shredder at an office-supply store for less than $50, and it's worth it. What should you shred? Preapproved credit card

offers, convenience or balance-transfer checks from
your credit card company, and any other mail or
documents with account or credit card numbers or
other personal information. When in doubt, shred
it.

- Don't respond to online or phone solicitations for
your Social Security number, bank-account information, or other personal details. This is called
phishing, and it's a very popular form of identity
theft. The thief will design an e-mail—and often an
e-mail address—that mimics one from a bank, credit
card company, or a business like PayPal or UPS. It
will direct you to a fake Web site, also designed after
whatever company the thief is mimicking, that asks
you to input sensitive account information or personal details such as your Social Security number.
Once you do, the thief has your information. A good
general rule of thumb: No bank, lender, or store will
send you an e-mail or even call you asking for personal information. Don't fall for it. When in doubt,
pick up the phone and call the company to verify
the authenticity of the e-mail or call.

- Install a firewall on your computer. If you're like me,
you use a DSL or cable modem that leaves you con-
nected to the Internet at all times. Great for conve-

nience; not so great for security. If you don't have some kind of protection, thieves can plant a pro-gram or virus in your machine and access the infor-mation on your hard drive. To stop this from happening, you need to install a firewall, which ba-sically functions like the lock on your home, and antispam/antivirus software. Be sure to keep them updated as well. Norton and McAfee are two well-known brands.

- Be selective about what you carry in your wallet and handbag. A good general rule of thumb is to carry only what you absolutely need to have with you. If you have a few credit cards, limit it to one on a daily basis. Leave the Social Security card at home. Don't keep your bank-account numbers and pass-words in your wallet. And take a general inventory of what is in there, so if your wallet is lost or stolen, you'll know what is missing.

- If you do fall victim to identity theft, the first thing you want to do is put a fraud alert on your credit file. You can do this by contacting one of the three credit-reporting agencies: Experian, Equifax, and TransUnion. Once you do, that agency is required by law to contact the other two. The fraud flag sig-nals to creditors that they need to take additional steps to confirm the identification of anyone who applies for credit in your name.

Next, you want to contact the creditors with whom the fraudulent accounts were opened, whether that's a credit card company (in most cases, it is), a bank, or a retailer. Request to have the accounts closed, and follow up in writing via certified mail to seal the deal.

After you've done that, head to your local police department and file a police report. This is so important, because having a copy of the police report will help legitimize your claims. You should also file a complaint with the FTC, which collects complaints and makes them available to police departments so that they can connect the dots and catch repeat offenders. Print the complaint form, because along with the police report, it can be used to dispute illegitimate accounts and make debt collectors stop collecting on fraudulent debts.

Throughout the whole process, you want to be sure to keep a record of the complaints you've filed, letters you've sent to the credit bureaus, and any other cor-respondence related to the identity theft. That way you have backup should you ever need it.

Letter to Dispute Information on Your Credit Report

Date
Your name
Your address
Your Social Security number

Name of credit-reporting agency
Address
Attn: Complaint Department

Dear Sir or Madam:

I am writing to dispute inaccurate information in my credit record. The creditor is [*name*] and the account number is [*xxx*].

This item, dated [*day/month/year*], is [*inaccurate* or *incomplete*] because [*I did not purchase the product* or *the amount is inaccurate* or *there is a mathematical error* or *the product or service was not delivered as agreed*]. I am requesting that the item be [*deleted from* or *corrected on*] my credit report.

A copy of my credit report with the disputed item highlighted and circled is attached. I am also enclosing [*any supporting documentation such as payment records*]. I am also requesting that this letter be kept on file as a permanent part of my credit record.

continued

Please investigate this matter with the creditor in question and [*delete* or *correct*] the disputed items as soon as possible. If you have any questions, I can be reached at [*day- and nighttime phone numbers*]. Thank you for your prompt attention.

Sincerely,

[*Your signature*]
[*Your typed name*]

Enclosures [*list attached items*]

Letter to Be Attached to Your Credit Report

Date

Name of lender
Address of lender

Dear Sir or Madam:

I am applying for a mortgage/loan with your company, and I am writing to explain the [*missed loan payment/bankruptcy/default/ other credit problem*] on my credit report. The information in question is circled on the attached copy of my credit report.

[*Explain what happened and why you were in financial difficulty: because of unemployment, illness, or other reasons.*] Fortunately, this problem has now been corrected [*because you found a job, etc.*]. On my credit report, you will notice that I have now amassed a [*year or however long*] track record of on-time payments, and have no other outstanding credit issues. In addition, I do not anticipate a recurrence of this problem in the future.

Please attach this letter to my loan-application file. I hope you will take this explanation into consideration when reviewing my application.

If you need further explanation or information, please do not hesitate to contact me at the address below or by phone [*daytime and evening phone numbers*].

Sincerely,

[*Your signature*]
[*Your typed name*]
[*Your address*]
[*City, state, zip*]

The Debt Diet

A few months ago, a woman came up to me on the soccer field and broke into tears. "I can't pay my bills," she confided. "I already refinanced the mortgage. But I've been so bad about paying on time in the past that I can't get low interest rates anymore. I don't know what to do. I feel like my life is completely falling apart."

Debt can be like that, I assured her, just as I've assured the many other people who have come up to me in airports, malls, doctors' offices, and hotel lobbies. It can be overwhelming, intimidating, and shameful. It can be isolating, making you feel like you haven't a friend in the world. The silver lining about hitting bottom like this—and this is what I told her—is that there's nowhere to go but up. She recognized her problem; she was ready to do something about it. And she wanted to do it today.

For many people, taking the time to methodically work your way through the steps to find your $10 a day will absolutely do the trick. Others, though—like my friend from the soccer field—are ready to go cold turkey. They need a jump-start, a quick fix, a shortcut. If you're one of them, the Debt Diet is for you.

What makes great diets like South Beach or Weight Watchers work is that they're simple. If you cut carbs or count points, you lose weight. The Debt Diet is similarly easy to remember and similarly easy to stick to. You'll see success early, feeling the weight of your debt burden rolling off your back as if it were pounds on the scale. And that easy loss will inspire you to do more . . . and more . . . and more (eventually adopting some of the important changes that have thousands of Americans living the *Pay It Down!* way).

Here's what you need to do:

Understand why you want this. Getting out of debt is going to require some trade-offs and sacrifice. Just like when you're off a diet, you have to want to get into the skinny pants more than you want the piece of chocolate cake; you have to understand why you want the shrinking credit card balance more than you want the skirt or the sconces or the baseball tickets or the three-course meal in your favorite restaurant. This is not necessarily easy. That item of clothing or plate of fettuccine Bolognese or whatever it is you're hankering for represents some immediate gratification: You buy it now, you can wear it tomorrow; you order it now, you'll have a full belly in thirty minutes.

Nobody gets that sort of rush from *not* spending money. But you will get, I promise, a sense of personal satisfaction and accomplishment (and maybe a hint of smug superiority) when you open the Visa bill and see that your balance is smaller. And you will deserve that. But you need to understand what it will mean to you to owe less money. I've done considerable research into this, so I can give you a glimpse. Then you can fill in your personal reasons.

- You will feel safer! Owing more than you can afford to owe gives you the feeling that your life—your house, your car, your rug (literally)—can be pulled out from under you at any time. You fear you may have to give it back. And that's a reasonable fear.

Cars do get repossessed. Homes do get foreclosed upon. People do have to file bankruptcy. But the secret is that banks really do not want your homes or your cars, and they rarely take the homes or the cars of people who are making progress repaying their debts, even if they're doing it slower than they originally intended. When you are repaying your debts, you no longer have to fear these things. So you will sleep better at night.

- You will feel more in control! Think about the last time you were on a diet and you sat in a restaurant with your friends, watching them make their way through the bread basket while you ate . . . nothing. How did you feel? Not hungry, I'm sure. Instead, you felt powerful, in control. Knowing that you can decide you don't have to have something just because you want it—and then following up on that decision by *not* eating it or *not* buying it—is an incredible feeling.

- You will have a better relationship with your spouse or partner! Money is the thing that couples fight about most—and debt (racking it up, not paying it off, lying about how much you have) is the particular line item that causes the most problems. When you're up front with the love of your life about how

much debt you have and the fact that you're moving in the right direction, it helps you work together
to build the life you really want.

- You will be happier! Bottom line, that's the truth.
People who have a grip on their debt are happier—
they worry less about their kids, their jobs, their
friendships, their weight and appearance, and their
lives overall. They feel more useful and confident.
Their self–esteem is higher.

- Getting out of debt will make me feel _____
_____!

Define your goal. If this were a weight–loss plan, one of
your first steps would be to figure out how much
weight you want to lose and how much time you have
to lose it. Perhaps the answer is ten pounds in time for
your high school reunion in two months. Or twenty
pounds so you can get into a bathing suit next summer. Think about your debt in the same way. Do you
need to pay back a $10,000 home equity line of credit
before you start making college–tuition payments
next fall? Or $5,000 on your credit card before you get
married because you haven't told (and don't want to)
your spouse–to–be about your pricey shoe fetish? Be
specific.

How much debt do I have?_____

_____

How many months do I have to pay it back?_____

_____

Do some math. Just as shedding ten or twenty pounds seems impossible and intimidating, getting rid of thousands of dollars in debt when you're only earning hundreds of dollars a week seems hopeless and ridiculous as well. Why even start when there's no doubt you're going to fail? That's where *good* diets (unlike *fad* diets) step in to help. They tell you on page two that you're succeeding if you shed a pound or two a week. Lose weight consistently at that pace and you'll absolutely be ten pounds lighter at your high school reunion. You can buy any bathing suit you want next summer. So let's do the same with your money. Divide your total debt by the months you have to repay it and you get:

How much debt am I trying to pay back a month?

_____

You'll notice I said *trying* to pay back. That was intentional. Just like losing *some* weight is better than losing no weight, eliminating *any* debt is a definite step in the right direction.

Memorize the mantras. There are three questions that people on the Debt Diet have to memorize:

Do I need it?
Why do I want it?
Can I afford it?

You're going to have to ask them of yourself again and again and again. And if you don't get a satisfactory answer—a defensible answer—then when it comes to spending money you are going to walk away.

Learn the rules. Okay, here come the tactical changes. Just as there are certain things you're not supposed to eat on the Zone diet or with Jenny Craig, the Debt Diet has some ground rules. There are some things you're going to start doing and other things you're not going to do anymore, and there are situations you're not going to put yourself in. On the Debt Diet, there are nine rules to guide your spending, and another four for how you're going to pay your bills—a baker's dozen all together.

1. Use debit, not credit. When you're using a debit card, you can't spend money you don't have.

2. Slim down your wallet. Take all but one credit card out of your wallet. That credit card is there for emergencies only. Take a piece of paper and write—in big letters—FOR EMERGENCIES ONLY on that piece of paper. Wrap the paper around the card and secure it with a rubber band. I am not kidding. The fact that you have to read this and unwrap the card just to use it will force you to think twice. (As for your other credit cards, you can do a number of things to get them out of your line of sight: Put them in a drawer or the freezer, or send them to your mother. If you are one of those people who have your credit card numbers memorized, call your card company, report the card stolen, and ask for a replacement. Do not memorize the new number. Again, I am totally serious.)

3. No online shopping. Shopping online is the downfall of insomniacs and people who are bored at work. It's way too easy. Push a button and whatever you want is yours. Even if you decide you don't want the item, you will spend money you don't have in shipping to return it.

4. One restaurant per day. If you are eating dinner out, you will bring lunch and eat breakfast at home. If you're craving breakfast at your favorite diner, you'll make lunch and dinner for yourself. (*Note:* McDonald's is a restaurant. So is Starbucks.)

5. Shop with a list. The folks at *Real Simple* magazine did a study on women who believe they are successful, and they found that successful women are list makers. Once you make the list, stick to it. If it's not on the list, you don't need it.

6. Shop for groceries once a week. Decide what you're going to make for dinner—all week—then buy everything you need. This will allow you to use the same bunch of broccoli that you serve as a side dish on Tuesday in a stir-fry on Friday. The reason our food expenditures have gone through the roof is because we don't decide what we want for dinner until four o'clock in the afternoon, then we go to the store on the way home (when we're hungry) and buy ingredients we don't need (because they're already in the pantry).

7. If you're wavering, put the item on hold. If you're still thinking about it twenty-four hours later, you can go back and get it then.

8. Return with abandon. You will suffer more buyer's remorse on this diet than you're used to. If you don't want it when you get home, take it back. Save all receipts for this purpose.

9. Make no more than one ATM visit a week. Cash is even easier to blow through than plastic. Decide how much cash you want to spend each week, take it out on a Monday, and divvy it into seven parts. That's how much to carry with you. If you spend less than your allocation on a single day, you can carry it over and use it for a little splurge. (See planned cheating, next page.)

10. Pay your bills as they come in, rather than all at once. The bottom line is this: People who pay their bills as they come in have more in savings and less in debt, and they're happier. It's a powerful habit to adopt.

11. Pay more than the minimum. Making the minimum payments is a sure way to stay in credit card debt for decades. I would like you to pay much more than the minimum, of course. But mostly it's important for you to get in the habit of paying more than the minimum. If you can pay only $10 more the first month, do it. Then increase it to $20, $50, $100, and so on.

12. Pay off the most expensive debts first. You'll get out of debt fastest by paying off those creditors that are costing you the most money first. If you have lots of cards with similarly high rates and one or two are more maxed out then the rest, focus on those maxed-out cards first, because doing so will improve your credit score—and that will allow you to borrow more inexpensively in the future.

13. Bank online. If you're a believer, as I am, that time is the new money, then paying your bills online saves you a lot of it. Surveys show it takes two hours a month to pay bills by hand. Doing it online takes fifteen minutes. But make sure you find a bank that will give you online banking services for free.

Allow Yourself Planned Cheats. Okay, let's just acknowledge up front that you are not going to be able to follow this plan to the letter. I certainly wouldn't be able to. That's why, like a good diet, in which one piece of great chocolate can save you from an entire weekend of overeating, on this plan you're allowed occasional splurges as well.

Weekly splurges come from whatever cash you've

been able to stockpile. If you put $20 in your wallet every day and spend only $14 of it, then by the weekend you'll have an extra $36. Add that to your $20 on a Saturday and go out for a nice dinner with your friends.

Monthly splurges come after you've been successful in eliminating a chunk of debt. Keep track of how much you've paid back over the course of a month, then take 5 to 10 percent of it and buy something you've been wanting to buy or do something you've been wanting to do.

Knowing which little splurges will feel the best isn't always easy. That's why it's important to monitor your reaction to things as you spend your money these days. Whenever you buy something, whether it's a pair of shoes, a magazine on the newsstand, a ticket to the movies, or a weekend in a nice hotel, take note of how that purchase makes you feel and how long the feeling lasts. Research has shown that spending money on experiences usually brings more satisfaction than spending money on things. Why? Because experiences grow in the retelling (often because you embellish them), whereas things tend to pale. This is an important lesson to pass on to your kids. I recently spent $36 on a wooden sign that reads THE MOST IMPORTANT THINGS IN LIFE AREN'T

THINGS. It hangs in my kitchen as a reminder to me—and also to them—that friends and family are what matter most. And of all the things in my carefully pulled-together house, this is the one that causes people to say, "I want one of those."

Rally Your Support. As I said earlier, I know that being in debt is embarrassing. It is uncomfortable. You don't want to talk about it. But if you're going to succeed on this diet, you're going to need the support of your friends, your spouse, and your family. So, I want you to start to share with them, one by one, the fact that you've taken on more debt than you like. Tell them you're trying really hard to pay back the money so you hope they'll understand if you're trying not to spend, and you hope they'll encourage you to succeed. Your true friends will start suggesting meeting for a low-cost coffee instead of a high-priced lunch—or even better, a no-cost walk in the park. They'll start sharing their tricks for not overspending. And don't be surprised: It won't be long before they start sharing their money-related troubles with you.

Ready Your Defenses. Having your friends on your side is important. But when you're on austerity in a world

that believes shopping is a sport, you'll need to be able
to get yourself out of a jam occasionally as well.

You'll need ways to spend money without spending
too much money. Weddings. Birthday parties. Holidays.
Tips during the holidays. Creativity is your friend here.
Try splitting the cost of a gift with a friend or two. If
your siblings or coworkers always exchange gifts at
Christmas, suggest a grab bag (buying for one person
is always less costly than buying for ten), and tack on a
price limit for good measure. (Don't worry, your cohorts
will be *relieved*.) When it comes to tips, you can either
give as much money as you can afford with a lovely
note (the important thing, etiquette experts emphasize,
is the thanking, not the amount), or you can do what
I've done when I've felt strapped: You can bake. Or
babysit. Or dog-walk. Or tutor. You can give of your
time. Finally, you can let yourself off the hook. I don't
care if there are three showers and an engagement party
for your girlfriend's upcoming wedding. You only have
to give her one gift.

You'll need an arsenal of excuses for not spending
your money. I want you to practice saying the following
things. Practice them in front of a mirror until you can
get them out believably, without smirking, and without
tearing up.

That's not worth the money.
I saw that on sale last week at Loehmann's, T. J. Maxx, etc.
Vogue *says that's so last year.*
I'm not really hungry.
I'd love to but I have plans that night.
I already have one just like it at home.
I've already used up all my vacation days.

Unfortunately, even with all of those fabulous truths (and they *are* truths) in your back pocket, I promise you that one day soon you will find yourself in this tough situation: You and five of your friends will go out for dinner. They will all have drinks, appetizers, entrées, and dessert. You will have a glass of water and a salad. You will use the "I'm not hungry" line and because you are now able to say it so effortlessly, none of your friends will think different. But when the check comes, someone at that table will expect to split it six ways.

You can handle this one of two ways. If you're brave, you can simply say, "We all ordered different things. Why don't we just pay for what we ordered?" Then circulate the check and hope everyone is able to compute their own tip. If you're not so brave, pick your best friend at that table, explain the situation to her, and ask her to do your bidding for you. It's a lot easier for someone to argue that someone else deserves to pay less than to do it on your own behalf.

Monitor Your Progress. A scale is such a great tool to have around because it allows you to see how you're doing on your quest to lose weight. You can do the same with your finances by doing the following:

- Keep a Debt Diary. In Step 4 I go through a plan for tracking your spending and why this is so important. As long as you're on the Debt Diet, this is absolutely crucial. Pick up a small notepad, tuck it in your pocketbook, and write down everything you spend—every dollar, every dime. At the end of the day, total your expenditures. You'll see them slowly but surely start to tail off.
- Open your financial statements. Your bank and credit card statements are your monthly weigh-ins. They're the indicators for how far you've come and how fast you've done it. I know the temptation is to just shove these things in a drawer; after all, they've brought bad news in the past. Don't do this anymore. Now the news they contain will be positive.
- Bank online. I am not a great fan of shopping on-

line, but banking online has changed my life. Truth be told, I have bounced some checks in the past. I have used my overdraft protection (and paid a $35 fee plus interest). That hasn't happened since I started banking online. Since I started banking online I can see, every day if I want, the movement of my money. If I feel like I'm a little flush, I can send some extra money to the credit card company in between statements. (I know I owe the money, they'll be happy to receive it, and by forwarding it to the card company I eliminate any opportunity to spend it.) And, if you're married and have joint accounts, banking online creates transparency. It allows both of you to keep tabs on when the money is coming in, when it's going out, and where it's going. That way you can discuss your spending patterns before things disintegrate into a huge fight.

- Monitor your credit score. If one of your goals of going on the Debt Diet is to improve your credit score so that you can refinance your mortgage, car loan, or student loan, or get credit cards at lower interest rates, you'll want to keep a close eye on your credit score. All three of the major credit bureaus and FICO (the company that cooks the score for the bureaus) offer services that allow you to monitor your score and its progress in real time. For more about this see Steps 3 and 11.

Get help if you aren't succeeding on your own. What you're taking on isn't easy. In fact, it's downright hard. And you may find that you're having trouble doing it alone. If that's the case, get some help. You may find that having a friend going through the same challenges at the same time is sufficient. Or you may want to consult a pro—one of the reputable credit counselors available to help you consolidate your debts and lower your interest rates. You'll find more information on them on page 177.

And, as always, if you have questions or problems, or if you've stumbled upon a solution you think might be helpful to other people, I want to hear about it. Send me an e-mail through my Web site, jeanchatzky.com. I'm in your corner. And I'm here to help.

Afterword: Congratulations!

Here you are, at the end of *Pay It Down!* I hope that along the way you were able to free up some cash and put it where it would do you the most good. I hope that you leave this book—and this exercise—feeling more optimistic about your financial future.

I look forward to hearing how you're doing. Your stories guide me as I work to explore the financial successes and problems of people all across the country (and to come up with creative solutions to the latter). So please let me know by writing me through jeanchatzky.com. I'll do my best to answer as many of your letters as I possibly can.

And remember, managing your money isn't rocket science. It's making good choices, developing good habits, and sticking to them. I know you can do it. I have faith in you.

Jean Chatzky

Acknowledgments

A big thank-you to all the people who helped pull this book (and the coordinating projects at *Money* magazine and at NBC's *Today*) together. I couldn't have done it without you: Richard Pine, Adrian Zackheim, Richard Heller, Heidi Krupp, Stephanie Land, Bob Safian, Denise Martin, Sheryl Tucker, Eric Schurenberg, Tom Touchet, Betsy Alexander, Patricia Luchsinger, Nancy Kay, Richard Liebner, Carrie Cook, Cybele Weisser, Will Weiser, Amy Wolfcale, Amy Mahfouz, Allison Sweet, Megan Casey, Kimberly Gaynor, Lysa Price, Andrew Federici, Sue Basalla, Jenny Baird, and Carolyn Bigda. I'm grateful to the experts who shared their knowledge: Scott Mitic, Keith Gumbinger, Scott Bilker, Robert D. Manning, Steve Tripoli, Elizabeth Warren, Craig Watts, Ryan Sjoblad, and John Ulzheimer. Thanks, too, to the people who are always on my side: Diane and Ken Adler, Jan and Dave Fisher, Elisa and Jamie Brickell, Kathy and Arlen Goldberg, Rob Densen, Wally Konrad, Nancy Pine, Lisa Greene, Susan Kleinman

Wechsler, Debi Epstein, Marc Fried, Marcia Meyers, and, of course, my family: the Shermans, the Chatzkys, the Lindes, the Meyers, and the Nelsons. And lastly, an additional round of thanks to the folks who helped with the update: Arielle McGowen, Sarah Compo, Adrienne Schultz, Michael Falcon, and Eliot Kaplan.

Dear Reader:

If you've gotten through the book and you feel like you still need a helping hand to conquer your debt, I've created a new online resource to help. Or if you've "cheated" and turned to this page before finishing the book, the online program can help you simultaneously— even if you aren't ready to start using the ideas. This online resource can also help your spouse or partner get ready to take on this task—which is crucial if one of you is ready and the other is not.

As you know, I like solutions that have been proven successful. I like evidence. I like data. So I formed a partnership with a company called Pro-Change. It was formed by scientists and university professors who have, for decades now, studied and researched behavior change. Their approach has helped tens of thousands of people quit smoking, exercise regularly, eat healthy, and manage stress. And now, we've combined their science with my debt-reduction strategies to help you. No matter how ready you are to start reducing your debt, using the right strategies at the right time can help you adopt and stick with the good habits in *Pay It Down!*

At www.jeanchatzky.com/debtdiet you'll find a link to the program. Then, please let me know how you're doing. I want to help keep you moving in the right direction.

Let's pay it down together!

Jean

Index